Mastering Skills for the TOEFL® iBT

Advanced | **SPEAKING**

Mastering Skills for the TOEFL® iBT: Speaking

Patrick Yancey • Moraig Macgillivray • Casey Malarcher

© 2006 Compass Publishing

Acquisitions Editor: Casey Malarcher
Development Editors: Garrett Byrne, David Charlton, Chan-hee Park
Contributing Writer: Michael Pederson
Recording Manager: Wendy Oh
Recording Assistant: Elisa Ha
Cover/Interior Design: Design Plus

email: info@compasspub.com
http://www.compasspub.com

ISBN: 978-1-59966-010-3

20 19 18 17 16 15 14 13 12 11 10 9 8 7 6 5 4
09 08 07

Mastering Skills for the TOEFL® iBT

iBT

Advanced

Patrick Yancey · Moraig Macgillivray · Casey Malarcher

SPEAKING

Compass Publishing

Table of Contents

Introduction

What to Expect on the TOEFL® Test

The TOEFL® test (Test of English as a Foreign Language) is an Internet-based test designed to assess English proficiency in non-native speakers who want to achieve academic success as well as effective communication. Most people take the TOEFL® test to gain admission into universities and colleges where instruction is in English. Additionally, many employers, government agencies, etc. use the scores to determine a person's English ability. It is not meant to test academic knowledge or computer ability, and as such, questions are always based on materials found in the test (computer tutorials are available for those not familiar with the PC). We have designed this practice book to be as similar as possible to the actual computer-based test in format and appearance in order to better prepare you for the TOEFL® test.

The TOEFL® test, like this series, is divided into four sections: reading, listening, speaking, and writing.

Major Changes in the Internet-Based TOEFL® (iBT)

- **General**
  - ⇨ The test measures all four language skills equally; a speaking section is included.
  - ⇨ The Test of Spoken English® (TSE®) will now be part of the TOEFL® test. Test takers will no longer take the TSE® as a separate test.
  - ⇨ The order of sections in the test are as follows:
    > Reading
    > Listening
    > (10-minute break)
    > Speaking
    > Writing
  - ⇨ The test is approximately four hours long and can be taken in one day.
  - ⇨ Tests are administered through the Internet in test centers around the world.
  - ⇨ Unlike past tests, there is no structure section.
  - ⇨ Note-taking is allowed in every section.
  - ⇨ The test is a linear exam, not computer adaptive; each test taker receives the same range of questions.
  - ⇨ The scores will be viewed online.

- **Reading/Listening**
  - ⇨ Passages for Reading and Listening are longer than those in the CBT (See introduction of individual sections for further details).

Speaking/Writing

⇨ Tasks for Speaking and Writing include integrated questions that require more than one skill to complete, i.e., reading and/or listening, then speaking or writing.

⇨ For the speaking section, test takers speak into a microphone, and their responses are digitized and sent to the ETS Online Scoring Network.

⇨ For the writing section, test takers must type their responses.

The New Test Format

Section	Number of Questions	Time (minutes)	Score
Reading	3–5 passages • 12–14 questions each • 700 words per passage	60–100	30 points
Listening	4–6 lectures • 6 questions each • 500–800 words (4–6 min.) 2–3 conversations • 5 questions each • 400–500 words (2–3 min.)	60–90	30 points
BREAK		10	
Speaking	2 independent tasks • 1 personal experience • 1 preference/choice 2 integrated tasks (Read-Listen-Speak) • Reading 100 words • Conversation 200 words (1–2 min.) • Lecture 200–300 words (1–2 min.) 2 integrated tasks (Listen-Speak) • Conversation 200 words (1–2 min.) • Lecture 200–300 words (1–2 min.)	20	30 points

Writing	1 independent task (same as TWE®)
	1 integrated task (Read-Listen-Write)
	  - Reading 250–300 words
	  - Lecture 250–300 words (2 min.)
		50	30 points

How this book is organized

There are four main sections and one practice test in this book.

Introduction   Understanding what each section requires you to do
Chapter 1   Practicing organizing and synthesizing information
Chapter 2   Developing coherence
Chapter 3   Focusing on clarity of speech
Practice Test   Practicing with questions designed according to the real test format

Test-taking and study tips

The only way to be certain of an excellent TOEFL® test score is to be able to read, write, understand, and speak English like an educated native speaker. You have no doubt been developing your ability in these areas for many years now. Unfortunately, this is not something one can accomplish by studying in the traditional way. However, research conducted over the years by applied linguists, psychologists, and educators has yielded a considerable amount of information on the best methods for refining these skills for the purposes of standardized tests. By keeping the following test-taking tips in mind, you can optimize your study habits and achieve the highest possible scores with the level of language proficiency you have developed.

General study tips:

- Prepare a study area for yourself. This should include the following:
    ⇨ A comfortable chair and spacious table/desk
    ⇨ Suitable lighting
    ⇨ Good ventilation and air quality; an open window or a house plant are good ideas
    ⇨ An area free of distractions such as outside noises/television/radio (unless of course you are using the television/radio to study listening)
    ⇨ Proper space to keep all the materials you will need when studying, such as books, paper, pens/pencils, a tape recorder or other recording device, and if possible, a computer with Internet access

- Study regularly over a long period of time. Do not study to the point of physical/mental exhaustion, as this has been shown to be ineffective in retaining information.

- "Cramming," i.e., studying intensely for long periods before an exam, is less effective, as it strains your general health and well-being and does not lead to good long-term retention of information/skills.

- Psychologists have discovered a principle called "state-specific memory." This means you remember things better in the same conditions that you learned them. So, for example, if you always study math at night, you will do better on a math exam at night. Use this concept to your advantage. If you know when and under what conditions you will take the TOEFL® test, simulate these in your study environment and habits. For example, if you will take the TOEFL® test on a Sunday afternoon from your computer at home, then make it a point to study at this computer on Sunday afternoons.

- Be well rested on the day of the exam. Do not stay up all night studying. Also, eat healthy foods including fruits and vegetables.

- Be relaxed and confident. Do the best that you can and do not worry excessively about any mistakes or uncertainties.

Registering for the TOEFL® test

Students must get registration information for the TOEFL® test. Registration information can be obtained online at the ETS website. The Internet address is www.ets.org/toefl. The website provides information such as testing locations, costs, and identification requirements. The website also provides other test preparation material.

The registration information, such as the test center location, identification requirements, and costs, will vary depending on the country in which you take the test. Be sure to follow these requirements carefully. If you do not have the proper requirements in order, you may not be able to take the test. Remember that if you register online, you will need to have your credit card information ready.

What TOEFL® test scores can be used for

The primary use of TOEFL® test scores is for acceptance into institutions such as universities and colleges in which English is the primary language of instruction. As noted earlier in this introduction, a great number of universities and other institutions require a certain TOEFL® test score for admission. In fact, it is estimated that as many as 4,400 such institutions require TOEFL® test scores for admission.

The exact calculation of a TOEFL® test score is complicated and probably not necessary for the student to understand. It is helpful to know, however, that each section of the Internet-based test is worth the same amount of points. The highest possible score on the iBT is 120 points. Each particular institution, for example, a university, will have its own score requirements for admission. For that reason, it is very important to check with each institution individually to find out what its admission requirements are. For example, a passing score at one university may not be a passing score at another university. It is the responsibility of the student to find out what the requirements are for each institution.

Although the primary use of TOEFL® test scores is for admission into English language institutions, there are a number of other places that require TOEFL® test scores. For example, many government agencies require TOEFL® test scores to evaluate an applicant's English ability for employment. In addition, many companies and corporations worldwide may also request TOEFL® test scores for similar uses. Even language institutes may request TOEFL® test scores for use in placing students in the appropriate level of English instruction.

Certainly, doing well on the TOEFL® test is important in many ways. Remember, practice makes perfect. We hope that you will take full advantage of this practice book and study hard. Your hard work and dedication will provide you with the best opportunity to do well on the TOEFL® test and to meet your goals for the future.

Speaking

The prompts for speaking questions on the TOEFL® iBT can be categorized into six types:

Question	Time			
	Reading	Listening	Preparation	Speaking
Independent Q1			15 seconds	45 seconds
Independent Q2				
Integrated Q3	45 seconds	1-2 minutes	30 seconds	60 seconds
Integrated Q4				
Integrated Q5		1-2 minutes	30 seconds	60 seconds
Integrated Q6				

The purpose of the speaking section is to evaluate your ability to speak coherently both on your opinions and experiences as well as on information that you have read or have heard. The speaking questions fall into two categories, independent and integrated. For the two independent speaking questions, you should draw upon your own experience and knowledge. For the remaining four speaking questions, you will speak about what you read and/or hear. Your ideas need to be well-organized and the language you speak needs to be accurate enough to be easily understood.

In particular, each question type will require test-takers to organize their ideas and speak toward different goals:

Question	Task	Materials	Length	Tasks
1	Independent	none		Describe your experience.
2	Independent	none		Give your opinion and explain why you think this.
3	Integrated	Reading Conversation	100 words 200 words 60-90 seconds	Restate the opinion of the speaker and the examples used.
4	Integrated	Reading Lecture	100 words 200 words 60-90 seconds	Explain how the example from the lecture supports the passage.
5	Conversation-based	Conversation	300 words 90-120 seconds	Restate suggestions and tell which you think is better.
6	Lecture-based	Lecture	300 words 90-120 seconds	Summarize what you heard.

Study Tips for Speaking

- Master the North American English phonetic system as best you can. Pay special attention to difficult distinctions such as: b/v, f/p, r/l, s/th, j/z, s/sh, the vowel sounds in *bat/bet*, *it/eat*, and *shirt/short*. Also, practice pronouncing the diphthongs (combined vowels) as one short, continuous sound rather than two separate ones. These include the sounds in the following: *hey*, *bye*, *boy*, and *go*.
- Practice speaking with a North American inflection. This involves moving the lips and opening the mouth more and speaking more from the mouth and nose than from the back of the throat.
- Practice using the pauses and intonations you learn when studying for the listening section.
- Practice speaking at home. Use one of the independent writing topics as a speaking topic. Give yourself 15 seconds of preparation time. Use this time to think of your main idea and details/examples to support it. Speak for approximately 45 seconds on the topic. (Also practice with 30 seconds of preparation time and 1 minute of speaking time, as this will be the case for the integrated exercises.)

Test Management

You will speak into a microphone attached to a headset.

Independent Speaking questions come first.

You can take notes and then use your notes when preparing your response.

Check the time with the clock shown in the title bar.

How Speaking Will Be Scored

ETS graders will score test-takers' responses according to the following scale:

Score	General Description	Key Points
4	The response answers the question or prompt well. The speaker is easy to understand and there are only minor mistakes with grammar or pronunciation.	Fluent speech that is easy to understand and follow, appropriate use of grammar and vocabulary, ideas explained clearly
3	The response answers the question or prompt, but not all of the ideas are fully developed. The speaker can be understood, but there are some clearly noticeable mistakes in speaking.	At least two (2) of these problems: pronunciation, pace of speech, wrong word choice, limited use of grammar structures, or incorrect grammar
2	The response gives only a basic or minimal answer to the question or prompt. Most sentences can be understood, but some effort is required by the listener because speech is not fluent and pronunciation is not accurate. Some ideas are not clearly explained.	At least two (2) of these problems: speech is choppy (not fluent), mistakes in pronunciation, wrong word choice, only use basic grammar, poor use of grammar, only basic ideas are presented, explanation is absent or limited
1	The response is very short, does not show full understanding of the question or prompt, and is hard for the listener to understand.	At least two (2) of these problems: poor pronunciation, speech is choppy (not fluent), long or frequent pauses, poor grammar makes ideas difficult to understand, use of obviously practiced or formulaic expressions, lots of repetition of expressions in the prompt
0	There is no response or the response is not related to the question or prompt.	No response to grade or response is not related to the question or prompt

Chapter 1

Thinking and Speaking

Necessary Skills

- Describing a personal experience or expressing a personal preference
- Organizing ideas
- Expressing a clear topic statement and the supporting points
- Speaking clearly and accurately with knowledge of grammar, vocabulary, and pronunciation

Strategies

- Though preparation time is limited in the speaking portion of the test, it is nevertheless important to use this time in planning the organization of your response. In this way, your response will be more relevant and coherent. An organizational process for preparing your speech is detailed below. In each step, there are certain things that you need to keep in mind.

Process	Strategy
Read the question and understand the task	Be sure that you understand the question and what the question requires you to do.
Decide on the topic statement	Decide on the main idea or choose one of the positions. Use the relevant parts of the prompt in making up your topic statement.
Brainstorm and select supporting ideas	Quickly think of the supporting ideas from your experience. Choose those ideas that most clearly support your topic statement.
Organize the ideas	Arrange your ideas, putting them in order from most to least important.

Skill A Q1 Practice 1 – Personal Experience

Step 1

Read the question. Write down your answer and related key points in the blanks.

> Tell about a person you admire who had an influence on your life. What specific characteristics do you admire in this person and in what ways has he or she influenced you?

The person I admire most is _____ *lense* _____ *7x in cro* _____.
Basle Ca
not to gue up

Characteristics I admire: _____

_____

_____

Ways he/she has influenced me: _____

_____

_____

Read the related ideas and expressions below. Add at least two of your own.

Related Ideas and Expressions

mentor:

guide, role model, hero, _____, _____

admire:

respect, esteem, revere, _____, _____

influence:

inspire, affect, compel, _____, _____

characteristics:

perseverance, dignity, virtue, _____, _____

---

mentor *(n)*:
a respected person who guides and teaches

revere *(v)*:
to admire greatly

compel *(v)*:
to make somebody do something; to exert strong pressure or influence on

perseverance *(n)*:
the quality of continuing to work at something despite difficulties and challenges

virtue *(n)*:
the quality of moral excellence and righteousness; goodness

Now create your own response using words and expressions from Step 1. Use the prompts below to help you.

_____ is my _____ for several reasons. First, he/she _____

_____. That, however, is not the only reason I _____. He/She also

_____. When _____, it

changed my life. He/She inspired me to _____.

His/Her qualities of _____ compelled

me to _____.

Step 3

Listen to the sample response and compare it with your response above. Make notes about the differences you hear.

Notes

Step 4

Review the response you wrote in Step 2 and your notes in Step 3. Then close your book and give a response to the question below. Say the response slowly and clearly. Try to speak for at least 60 seconds.

Tell about a person you admire who had an influence on your life. What specific characteristics do you admire in this person and in what ways has he or she influenced you?

Skill A Q1 Practice 2 – Personal Experience

Step 1

Read the question. Write down your answer and related key points in the blanks.

> Describe a specific instance in which technology has helped you in your schoolwork. Include details in your description.

Type of technology that helped me: _____

Why I needed it: _____

How it helped: _____

What I would have to do without it: _____

Read the related ideas and expressions below. Add at least two of your own.

Related Ideas and Expressions

technology:

computers, gadgets, media, _____, _____

obstacle:

learning disability, dyslexia, hindrance, _____, _____

overcome:

beat, conquer, excel, _____, _____

help:

aid, assist, support, _____, _____

gadget *(n)*:
a small tool or appliance, often electronic

learning disability *(n phrase)*:
a disorder found in children of normal intelligence, causing difficulties in learning specific skills

dyslexia *(n)*:
a disorder marked by difficulty in recognizing the order of written letters and words, thus making reading a challenge

hindrance *(n)*:
a problem or impediment that slows the progress of

excel *(v)*:
to perform better than others or better than expected

Step 2

Now create your own response using words and expressions from Step 1. Use the prompts below to help you.

One _____ that has helped me with schoolwork is _____. To begin,

I _____

The _____ was of great assistance to me. It _____.

I used it _____. Without it, I _____

_____. Because of my _____, I was able to _____.

Step 3

Listen to the sample response and compare it with your response above. Make notes about the differences you hear.

Notes

Step 4

Review the response you wrote in Step 2 and your notes in Step 3. Then close your book and give a response to the question below. Say the response slowly and clearly. Try to speak for at least 60 seconds.

> Describe a specific instance in which technology has helped you in your schoolwork. Include details in your description.

Skill A Q1 Practice 3 – Personal Experience

Step 1

Read the question. Write down your answer and related key points in the blanks.

> Many children all over the world spend a great deal of time playing sports. Has your own experience with youth sports been positive or negative? Give specific reasons and details as to how playing sports has helped or harmed you.

Some sports I have practiced were: _____

_____

I feel that this has (helped/hurt) _____ me because:

Reason 1: _____

Details: _____

Reason 2: _____

Details: _____

Read the related ideas and expressions below. Add at least two of your own.

Related Ideas and Expressions

benefit:

gain, be better off, advantage, _____, _____

hurt:

hinder, negate, damage, _____, _____

important:

chief, crucial, integral, _____, _____

health:

endurance, strength, stamina, _____, _____

better off *(adj phrase)*:
in a better situation or condition

hinder *(v)*:
to impede; to slow the progress of

negate *(v)*:
to make ineffective; to counteract

chief *(adj)*:
main; principal

crucial *(adj)*:
very important; essential

stamina *(n)*:
the ability to perform exercise for a long period of time; endurance

Step 2

Now create your own response using words and expressions from Step 1. Use the prompts below to help you.

When I was a child, I used to _____. I feel that practicing

_____. The chief _____ was that competing in _____

_____. Playing _____

_____. _____, on the other hand, _____

_____. Developing a _____ when I was young

has _____.

Step 3

🎧 Listen to the sample response and compare it with your response above. Make notes about the differences you hear.

Notes

_____

_____

_____

_____

Step 4

Review the response you wrote in Step 2 and your notes in Step 3. Then close your book and give a response to the question below. Say the response slowly and clearly. Try to speak for at least 60 seconds.

Many children all over the world spend a great deal of time playing sports. Has your own experience with youth sports been positive or negative? Give specific reasons and details as to how playing sports has helped or harmed you.

Skill A Q2 Practice 1 – Personal Preference

Step 1

Read the question. Write down your answer and related key points in the blanks.

> Do you agree or disagree with the following statement? High schools should allow students to study the courses that students want to study. Use specific reasons and examples to support your opinion.

I agree/disagree with _____

Reason 1: _____

Example: _____

Reason 2: _____

Example: _____

Read the related ideas and expressions below. Add at least two of your own.

Related Ideas and Expressions

allow:

permit, let, give permission, _____, _____

control:

select, in charge, destiny, _____, _____

enjoy:

crave, find diverting, be interested in, _____, _____

course:

subjects, curriculum, path, _____, _____

in charge (adj phrase):
in control; able to lead and make choices

destiny (n):
the events that will occur in one's life; fate

crave (v):
to want strongly

diverting (adj):
entertaining; fun

curriculum (n):
the group of subjects studied at school and their schedule of study

Step 2

Now create your own response using words and expressions from Step 1. Use the prompts below to help you.

In my opinion, _____.

This ensures _____. If, for example,

_____.

In the long run, _____.

Obviously, if _____.

Step 3

Listen to two sample responses and compare them with your response above. Make notes about the differences you hear.

Notes

Step 4

Review the response you wrote in Step 2 and your notes in Step 3. Then close your book and give a response to the question below. Say the response slowly and clearly. Try to speak for at least 60 seconds.

Do you agree or disagree with the following statement? High schools should allow students to study the courses that students want to study. Use specific reasons and examples to support your opinion.

Skill A Q2 Practice 2 – Personal Preference

Step 1

Read the question. Write down your answer and related key points in the blanks.

> Some celebrities use their fame to influence society with their views. Some people are strongly affected by these celebrities, while other people believe the public should not pay attention to these views just because they come from rich and well-known members of society. With which opinion do you agree? Use specific reasons and examples to support your answer.

In my view, people _____ pay attention to the opinions expressed by celebrities.

Reason 1: _____

Example: _____

Reason 2: _____

Example: _____

Read the related ideas and expressions below. Add at least two of your own.

Related Ideas and Expressions

famous:

renowned, expert, erudite, _____, _____

opinions:

cynical, views, commentary, _____, _____

listen to:

pay attention to, heed, give credence to, _____, _____

influence:

sway, affect, persuade, _____, _____

expert (adj):
having great skill or knowledge

erudite (adj):
having or requiring a high level of knowledge or learning

cynical (adj):
skeptical; pessimistic

heed (v):
to listen to and follow the advice of

give credence to (v phrase):
to treat with respect and legitimacy; to believe and support

Step 2

Now create your own response using words and expressions from Step 1. Use the prompts below to help you.

Some celebrities _____, while others _____.

In my opinion, _____. After all,

_____.

Some _____.

However, _____.

Step 3

🎧 Listen to two sample responses and compare them with your response above. Make notes about the differences you hear.

Notes

Step 4

Review the response you wrote in Step 2 and your notes in Step 3. Then close your book and give a response to the question below. Say the response slowly and clearly. Try to speak for at least 60 seconds.

Some celebrities use their fame to influence society with their views. Some people are strongly affected by these celebrities, while other people believe the public should not pay attention to these views just because they come from rich and well-known members of society. With which opinion do you agree? Use specific reasons and examples to support your answer.

Skill A **Q2** Practice 3 – Personal Preference

Step 1

Read the question. Write down your answer and related key points in the blanks.

> Do you agree or disagree with the following statement? Children should be required to help with household tasks as soon as they are able to do so. Use specific reasons and examples to support your answer.

I believe children _____.

Reason 1: _____

Details: _____

Reason 2: _____

Details: _____

Read the related ideas and expressions below. Add at least two of your own.

Related Ideas and Expressions

required:

obligated, made to, forced, _____, _____

household tasks:

chores, housework, domestic work, _____, _____

help out:

pitch in, lend a hand, lift a finger, _____, _____

responsibility:

competency, maturity, diligence, _____, _____

chore (n):
a small piece of work often performed on a regular schedule

domestic (adj):
related to the house or home country

pitch in (v phrase):
to help others perform a certain task

lift a finger (v phrase):
to work; to make an effort

maturity (n):
the state of being responsible and adult-like

Step 2

Now create your own response using words and expressions from Step 1. Use the prompts below to help you.

Some children _____, while others _____.

I personally feel _____.

This _____ them _____. Children who _____

_____. Parents may think _____,

but in the long run, _____.

Step 3

Listen to two sample responses and compare them with your response above. Make notes about the differences you hear.

Notes

Step 4

Review the response you wrote in Step 2 and your notes in Step 3. Then close your book and give a response to the question below. Say the response slowly and clearly. Try to speak for at least 60 seconds.

> Do you agree or disagree with the following statement? Children should be required to help with household tasks as soon as they are able to do so. Use specific reasons and examples to support your answer.

Sample Responses

Skill A Independent Speaking: Organizing Speech

Q1 - Practice 1

Lance Armstrong is my role model for several reasons. First, he is a cyclist who has won the Tour de France seven times in a row. That, however, is not the only reason I respect this man. He also battled cancer. When I heard his story, it changed my life. Lance Armstrong inspired me to never give up on my dream of going to the Olympics, even though it may seem impossible. His qualities of endurance and perseverance compelled me to become a better athlete and a stronger person.

Q1 - Practice 2

One gadget that has helped me with schoolwork is my "reading pen." To begin, I have dyslexia, a learning disability that makes reading very difficult. The reading pen was of great assistance to me. It scans words on a page and reads them out loud to me. I used it every day to help me with my reading assignments. Without it, I would have spent hours reading my assignments and wouldn't have had time to study properly. Because of my reading pen, I was able to excel in school.

Q1 - Practice 3

When I was a child, I used to play soccer and baseball. I feel that practicing these sports helped me greatly. The chief benefit was that competing in these sports made my body healthy, instilling me with endurance and strength. Playing baseball developed my upper body strength for hitting and throwing. Soccer, on the other hand, provided me with lower body strength for kicking and stamina and endurance for playing full 90-minute games. Developing a strong, healthy body when I was young has been crucial in maintaining my health later in life.

Q2 - Practice 1
Opinion 1:

In my opinion, high school students should be required to follow a certain curriculum. This ensures students are exposed to a wide variety of subjects. If, for example, I had been permitted to select whatever courses I wanted, I would only have taken courses that I found diverting. In the long run, this would have limited my ability to pursue a medical career, which is what I'm doing now. Obviously, if I had been left to my own devices about choosing my courses, I would not be where I am today.

Opinion 2:

In my opinion, educators should let high school students decide which courses they want to study. This ensures that all students are in charge of their own destinies, and they should be permitted to determine their own academic paths. If, for example, a student prefers art to science, why should she waste her time studying science? In the long run, her efforts would be better spent on developing skills in a field that interests her. Obviously, if she has to direct part of her energy toward a course she doesn't like, she will have less time and energy to put toward her real interests.

Q2 - Practice 2

Opinion 1:

Some celebrities become rich and famous and then return very little to society, while others attempt to use their influence to raise public awareness of a special cause, such as environmentalism or human rights. In my opinion, we are all better off heeding the expert advice of professionals and officials. After all, how much can a pop star really know about solving problems in Africa? Some people say stars can do a lot if they get behind a particular cause, and there may be some truth to that. However, expecting an erudite opinion from a pop star about health issues in Nigeria is a different matter.

Opinion 2:

Some celebrities become rich and famous and then return very little to society, while others attempt to use their influence to raise public awareness of a special cause, such as environmentalism or human rights. In my opinion, the least the public can do is carefully consider these views. After all, a person living at the top of society probably has a much better view of it and can see problems that normal people cannot. Some cynics contend that people should ignore well-known artists when they express their thoughts on global issues. However, I attribute these views to jealousy.

Q2 - Practice 3

Opinion 1:

Some children begin helping out with household chores as soon as they are old enough, while others may never lift a finger. I personally feel that children should pitch in around the house as soon as possible. This teaches them the value of work and gives them a feeling of accomplishment and responsibility. Children who never have to assist around the house often become spoiled and grow up expecting others to do work for them. Parents may think they are helping their kids by doing their work for them, but in the long run, this is not the case.

Opinion 2:

Some children begin helping out with household chores as soon as they are old enough, while others may never lift a finger. I personally feel that childhood is a special time for learning and playing. This helps kids develop imagination, creativity, and social skills through interacting with friends. Children who have little time to enjoy childhood because they are doing work or chores are not given the opportunity to be young. Parents may think that they are teaching their kids responsibility, but in the long run, this lesson costs children more than it's worth.

Integrated Speaking: Synthesizing Information

Necessary Skills

- Understanding information in reading and listening passages
- Taking notes of important information and using this information in your spoken response
- Synthesizing background information with more specific information
- Synthesizing the information given in the reading and listening; using the points in the listening to highlight principles or differences in the reading
- Recognizing a speaker's purpose and attitude
- Paraphrasing information

Strategies

- An organizational process for responding to a prompt based on integrated material is detailed below. In each step, there are certain things that you need to keep in mind.

Process	Strategy
Read and listen	Take notes of the important information in the reading and listening passages.
Read the question and understand the task	Identify the relationship between the information from the listening passage and that from the reading passage. What aspects of each does the prompt want you to discuss?
Organize the ideas	Arrange the ideas from the listening and reading passages. Think of a topic sentence that reflects the information.

Skill B Q3 Practice 1 — Reading and Conversation

Read the following information. Write 5 keywords or key phrases that would be useful in explaining this passage to someone else. While reading, try to guess what the conversation will be about.

CONSTRUCTION ANNOUNCEMENT

The construction of the new Science Center will commence on March 8th next to Clemens Hall. So that classes will not be disturbed by the noise and commotion, all classes in Clemens Hall will be relocated to other buildings on campus. All professors will receive a memo advising them of their new class location and should relay the information to their students. We regret any inconvenience this might cause, but feel confident that the new Science Center will be well worth the disruption.

commence (v):
to begin; to start

commotion (n):
a large, confusing amount of noise and movement

relocate (v):
to move; to change the place of

relay (v):
to pass information one has received on to another person or group; to tell

disruption (n):
a break from a regularly scheduled activity; an unpleasant interruption

keywords /
key phrases

Cover the passage and look at the keywords and key phrases only. Restate the passage in your own words.

Step 2

Now listen to a conversation related to the passage in Step 1. As you listen, take notes on important information. Write down 5 keywords or key phrases that would be useful in explaining this information to someone else.

notes / keywords

hold off *(v phrase):*
to wait
distracting *(adj):*
causing loss of focus and concentration
cacophony *(n):*
a large amount of jarring, unpleasant sound
allay *(v):*
to provide relief; to make better
figure out *(v phrase):*
to make a final decision; to realize

Restate what you heard in the conversation using the notes or keywords you wrote above.

Step 3

Read the question. Circle the most important ideas in your notes, from both the reading and the listening. Write down the main points you need to speak about.

> The woman changes her opinion about the construction of the new Science Center. State her original opinion and her reasons for it. Then state why she changes her mind.

Original Opinion: The woman thinks _____.

Reason: _____.

Why she changes her mind: _____.

Step 4

Now create your own response using the information from your notes in Steps 1, 2, and 3. Use the prompts below to help you.

The woman thinks that _____ .

Her concern is _____ .

However, _____ .

When she learns this, _____ .

Step 5

🎧 Listen to the sample response and compare it with your response above. Make notes about the differences you hear.

Notes

_____

_____

_____

_____

Step 6

Review the response you wrote in Step 4 and your notes in Step 5. Then close your book and give a response to the question below. Say the response slowly and clearly. Try to speak for at least 60 seconds.

The woman changes her opinion about the construction of the new Science Center. State her original opinion and her reasons for it. Then state why she changes her mind.

Step 1

Read the following information. Write 5 keywords or key phrases that would be useful in explaining this passage to someone else. While reading, try to guess what the conversation will be about.

ANTI-SPAM POLICY

Commencing next week, a new anti-spam filter will scan all emails coming into the university network for unsolicited emails, a.k.a. spam. All emails sent to university accounts will be sorted into three categories: Spam, Potential Spam, and Safe. Naturally, safe email will go directly to the recipient's inbox. Conversely, if an incoming email is obviously spam, it will be blocked. Finally, if an email looks like it could be spam, it will be redirected to the recipient's bulk folder.

unsolicited (adj):
not requested; not asked for

a.k.a. (acronym):
also known as

recipient (n):
the person to whom an email or letter is sent; the person meant to receive something

redirect (v):
to change the direction of; to move to a place different from the originally intended place

bulk (adj):
being large in volume or quantity; related to mail sent to a large number of addresses simultaneously

keywords /
key phrases

_____

_____

_____

_____

_____

Cover the passage and look at the keywords and key phrases only. Restate the passage in your own words.

Now listen to a conversation related to the passage in Step 1. As you listen, take notes on important information. Write down 5 keywords or key phrases that would be useful in explaining this information to someone else.

notes / keywords

implement *(v)*:
to put in; to start using

abhor *(v)*:
to hate

from time to time *(adv phrase)*:
occasionally

incertitude *(n)*:
a doubt; a feeling of uncertainty

misidentify *(v)*:
to make an incorrect conclusion about the nature of something

Restate what you heard in the conversation using the notes or keywords you wrote above.

Step 3

Read the question. Circle the most important ideas in your notes, from both the reading and the listening. Write down the main points you need to speak about.

The woman expresses her opinion about the new anti-spam filter. The man expresses his concern about it. State the woman's opinion and the man's concern. Who changes his or her mind in the end and why?

Woman's opinion: The anti-spam filter is _____.

Reason: _____

Man's Concern: _____

_____ changes his/her mind.

Reason: _____

Step 4

Now create your own response using the information from your notes in Steps 1, 2, and 3. Use the prompts below to help you.

The man and the woman are discussing _____. The woman,

who hates _____, thinks it's _____ idea. The man, however,

_____.

The woman _____.

If an incoming email _____.

In the end, _____.

Step 5

Listen to the sample response and compare it with your response above. Make notes about the differences you hear.

Notes

Step 6

Review the response you wrote in Step 4 and your notes in Step 5. Then close your book and give a response to the question below. Say the response slowly and clearly. Try to speak for at least 60 seconds.

The woman expresses her opinion about the new anti-spam filter. The man expresses his concern about it. State the woman's opinion and the man's concern. Who changes his or her mind in the end and why?

Skill B Q3 Practice 3 — Reading and Conversation

Step 1

Read the following information. Write 5 keywords or key phrases that would be useful in explaining this passage to someone else. While reading, try to guess what the conversation will be about.

SELWIDGE HALL LECTURE SERIES — JAMES BRENTWORTH

The Business and Information Technology faculties are proud to present this week's guest speaker, James Brentworth. James was only seventeen when he inaugurated his website, which has now grown into a multi-million dollar enterprise. James will speak on the topics of Internet business and the future of telecommerce from 7 p.m. to 8 p.m., Thursday night in Selwidge Hall. Students from all disciplines are welcome to attend, and the speech will be followed by a brief question-and-answer period.

faculty (n):
a branch of a university in charge of one field of study

inaugurate (v):
to begin; to launch

enterprise (n):
a business venture

telecommerce (n):
the field of business and banking done using telecommunications such as telephones or Internet

discipline (n):
a field of study; a major

keywords / key phrases

Cover the passage and look at the keywords and key phrases only. Restate the passage in your own words.

Step 2

🎧 Now listen to a conversation related to the passage in Step 1. As you listen, take notes on important information. Write down 5 keywords or key phrases that would be useful in explaining this information to someone else.

notes / keywords

> **extra credit** *(adj phrase):* related to assignments outside the regular course assignments and exams that are designed to allow students to increase their grades
>
> **whiz kid** *(n phrase):* a teenager or child with exceptional intelligence or achievements
>
> **counsel** *(n):* a series of suggestions; advice
>
> **freebie** *(n):* an event or item that costs nothing
>
> **beforehand** *(adv):* prior to an event

Restate what you heard in the conversation using the notes or keywords you wrote above.

Step 3

Read the question. Circle the most important ideas in your notes, from both the reading and the listening. Write down the main points you need to speak about.

> The man asks the woman for some information about an assignment. What does the woman tell him, and how does he react?

The man wants information on: _____

The woman tells him he can: _____

The man's opinion of the assignment is that: _____

_____.

Reason 1: _____.

Reason 2: _____.

The man will: _____.

■ **Step 4**

Now create your own response using the information from your notes in Steps 1, 2, and 3. Use the prompts below to help you.

First, the man _____ .

The woman then _____ .

The man is _____ about _____ for _____ reasons.

First, _____ .

In addition, _____ . Therefore, _____

_____ .

■ **Step 5**

🎧 Listen to the sample response and compare it with your response above. Make notes about the differences you hear.

Notes
```



```

■ **Step 6**

Review the response you wrote in Step 4 and your notes in Step 5. Then close your book and give a response to the question below. Say the response slowly and clearly. Try to speak for at least 60 seconds.

> The man asks the woman for some information about an assignment. What does the woman tell him, and how does he react?

Skill B Q4 Practice 1 — Reading and Lecture

Step 1

Read the following information. Write 5 keywords or key phrases that would be useful for explaining this passage to someone else. While reading, try to guess what the lecture will be about.

The Nash Equilibrium

One of the greatest contributions of renowned mathematician, John Nash, is the Nash Equilibrium. It describes situations in which competing parties maintain static strategies for success. Each competitor has a rational conception of the strategies of the other competitors, but no collusion takes place. Consequently, each competitor chooses a strategy for success based only on his or her best interests. Nevertheless, the continuation of each individual competitor's strategy also benefits the success of the competing parties. As a corollary, if one party decides to alter its strategy, all competing parties will suffer.

renowned *(adj)*:
famous; well known

equilibrium *(n)*:
a state in which things remain constant, or equal on two or more sides

static *(adj)*:
unchanging

collusion *(n)*:
the act of agreeing on a plan

corollary *(n)*:
a consequence that follows logically

keywords / key phrases

_____

_____

_____

_____

_____

Cover the passage and look at the keywords and key phrases only. Restate the passage in your own words.

Step 2

🎧 Now listen to a lecture related to the passage in Step 1. As you listen, take notes on important information. Write down 5 keywords or key phrases that would be useful in explaining this information to someone else.

notes / keywords

collision *(n)*:
the act of crashing, or colliding

oncoming *(adj)*:
moving towards

in essence *(adv phrase)*:
basically; essentially

delay *(n)*:
the condition of being later or slower than expected or desired; a postponement

pose *(v)*:
to put forward; to present

Restate what you heard in the lecture using the notes or keywords you wrote above.

Step 3

Read the question. Circle the most important ideas in your notes, from both the reading and the listening. Write down the main points you need to speak about.

> The professor describes an example of how the Nash Equilibrium applies to daily life. Explain the example and how it relates to the Nash Equilibrium.

Nash Equilibrium: _____

Professor's example: _____

How they relate: _____

Step 4

Now create your own response using the information from your notes in Steps 1, 2, and 3. Use the prompts below to help you.

The reading passage describes _____.

The professor expounds on _____.

This example _____. If _____

_____, then _____. That is to say, _____

_____.

Step 5

🎧 **Listen to the sample response and compare it with your response above. Make notes about the differences you hear.**

Notes

Step 6

Review the response you wrote in Step 4 and your notes in Step 5. Then close your book and give a response to the question below. Say the response slowly and clearly. Try to speak for at least 60 seconds.

The professor describes an example of how the Nash Equilibrium applies to daily life. Explain the example and how it relates to the Nash Equilibrium.

Skill B Q4 Practice 2 — Reading and Lecture

Step 1

Read the following information. Write 5 keywords or key phrases that would be useful for explaining this passage to someone else. While reading, try to guess what the lecture will be about.

The Black Plague

The Black Plague is the disease that swept through Europe in the 1300s, killing up to two thirds of the entire population. It would return once every generation or so for the next several hundred years. Eventually, the rise of germ theory found that this strain of the bubonic plague was caused by a bacterium called *Yersinia pestis*. This microorganism was spread from rats to humans via parasitic fleas. Improved public sanitation combined with the advent of antibiotics helped eradicate the disease in Europe.

sweep through *(v phrase)*:
to spread or move quickly across a given area

strain *(n)*:
a type

parasitic *(adj)*:
relating to living on another living thing without helping it

advent *(n)*:
the beginning; the coming of

eradicate *(v)*:
to destroy; to remove completely

keywords /
key phrases

_____

_____

_____

_____

_____

Cover the passage and look at the keywords and key phrases only. Restate the passage in your own words.

Now listen to a lecture related to the passage in Step 1. As you listen, take notes on important information. Write down 5 keywords or key phrases that would be useful in explaining this information to someone else.

notes / keywords

> **scrutiny (n):**
> the act of questioning and examining closely
>
> **culprit (n):**
> a guilty party; a cause
>
> **pandemic (n):**
> a widespread disease affecting many people
>
> **subsequent (adj):**
> following after in time
>
> **incubation (n):**
> the development of an infection from the time the microorganism enters the body until signs or symptoms first appear

Restate what you heard in the lecture using the notes or keywords you wrote above.

Step 3

Read the question. Circle the most important ideas in your notes, from both the reading and the listening. Write down the main points you need to speak about.

> The professor explains new theories and evidence about the Black Plague. Explain how the new theories and evidence relate to the common understanding of the plague and how it spread.

Common understanding: _____

New evidence 1: _____

New evidence 2: _____

New theories:

    1: _____

    2: _____

Step 4

Now create your own response using the information from your notes in Steps 1, 2, and 3. Use the prompts below to help you.

In the lecture, the professor _____

_____. The traditional theory _____

_____. First, _____

_____. Second, _____

_____. For these reasons, _____

_____.

Step 5

Listen to the sample response and compare it with your response above. Make notes about the differences you hear.

Notes

_____

_____

_____

_____

Step 6

Review the response you wrote in Step 4 and your notes in Step 5. Then close your book and give a response to the question below. Say the response slowly and clearly. Try to speak for at least 60 seconds.

The professor explains new theories and evidence about the Black Plague. Explain how the new theories and evidence relate to the common understanding of the plague and how it spread.

Skill B Q4 Practice 3 — Reading and Lecture

■ Step 1

Read the following information. Write 5 keywords or key phrases that would be useful for explaining this passage to someone else. While reading, try to guess what the lecture will be about.

The Great Zimbabwe Civilization

Around 450 A.D., Shona-speaking herders migrated to the high Zimbabwe plateau to escape the ravages of the tsetse fly. Between 1100 and 1450, the plateau was the site of the Great Zimbabwe civilization, with cities, a king, and an impressive stone wall 800 feet long and 32 feet high. The civilization thrived on cattle and the gold trade but began to break up in 1450 for unknown reasons. It was badly plundered by the British during colonial times but is now a popular tourist attraction.

herder (n):
a person who raises livestock, such as cattle, sheep, or goats

migrate (v):
to move in large numbers from one area to another

plateau (n):
a large, flat area of land

ravages (n):
a series of problems or damage

thrive (v):
to live successfully

keywords /
key phrases

_____

_____

_____

_____

_____

Cover the passage and look at the keywords and key phrases only. Restate the passage in your own words.

Now listen to a lecture related to the passage in Step 1. As you listen, take notes on important information. Write down 5 keywords or key phrases that would be useful in explaining this information to someone else.

notes / keywords

undermine (v):
to destroy the foundation of

commission (v):
to hire officially

plunder (v):
to destroy and steal from

contradict (v):
to state the opposite of; to question the validity of

dispel (v):
to prove a belief or opinion is false

Restate what you heard in the lecture using the notes or keywords you wrote above.

Step 3

Read the question. Circle the most important ideas in your notes, from both the reading and the listening. Write down the main points you need to speak about.

The professor describes archaeological investigations of the ruins on the Zimbabwe plateau. Describe the archaeologists' conclusions about the ruins and how they relate to the accepted history of the site today.

First British investigation: _____

Conclusion and result: _____

Further investigation: _____

Conclusion and result: _____

Accepted idea today: _____

Step 4

Now create your own response using the information from your notes in Steps 1, 2, and 3. Use the prompts below to help you.

The lecture _____.

The reading _____.

This evidence _____.

British officials, on the other hand, _____

_____. Their hired archaeologists _____

_____. Finally, _____

_____.

Step 5

🎧 Listen to the sample response and compare it with your response above. Make notes about the differences you hear.

Notes

_____

_____

_____

_____

_____

Step 6

Review the response you wrote in Step 4 and your notes in Step 5. Then close your book and give a response to the question below. Say the response slowly and clearly. Try to speak for at least 60 seconds.

> The professor describes archaeological investigations of the ruins on the Zimbabwe plateau. Describe the archaeologists' conclusions about the ruins and how they relate to the accepted history of the site today.

Skill B Independent Speaking: Synthesizing Information

Q3 - Practice 1

The woman thinks that the university ought to wait until summer before they start building the new Science Center. Her concern is that the classes in nearby buildings, specifically, her class at Clemens Hall, will be distracted by the noise from the construction. However, when she talks to the man, he tells her that the university is planning on relocating the classes in Clemens Hall to other buildings on campus. When she learns this, she is relieved, and changes her mind about waiting until summer to commence construction on the new building.

Q3 - Practice 2

The man and the woman are discussing a new anti-spam filter that will be installed at their university. The woman, who hates receiving spam, thinks it's a wonderful idea. The man, however, is concerned that the filter will make mistakes and accidentally block important mail. The woman assures him, though, that the filter has a safety feature. It only blocks mail that is obviously spam. If an incoming email looks suspicious, it is sent to the person's bulk folder. In the end, the man agrees that this system is probably safe and agrees with the woman that it is a good idea.

Q3 - Practice 3

First, the man asks the woman for information on an extra credit assignment for a Web Design class they are both in. The woman then refers him to an announcement about a guest speaker, reminding him that they can earn credit for attending the talk. The man is excited about the opportunity for two reasons. First, he thinks the guest speaker will provide useful advice for aspiring web designers. In addition, he is pleased that there's no charge for admission to the speech. Therefore, he will prepare some questions to ask the speaker and attend the speech to receive extra credit.

Q4 - Practice 1

The reading passage describes the Nash Equilibrium, a situation in competitions in which it is not in any competitor's interest to change strategy. The professor expounds on this idea by illustrating a real life example of the Nash Equilibrium. This example refers to drivers in rush hour traffic. If each driver is considered a competitor, and driving on one side of the road as the strategy, then it fits the Nash Equilibrium. That is to say, it is not in a driver's interest to change strategy, given that a collision could hinder the success of that driver, and coincidentally, the other drivers, too.

Q4 - Practice 2

In the lecture, the professor discusses new theories about the cause of the Black Plague, a disease that killed two-thirds of Europeans in the 14th century. The traditional theory that it was bubonic plague spread to people by fleas carried on rats does not match up with some new evidence. First, Iceland was severely affected despite the fact it had no rats. Second, the incubation period and spreading of the disease differed from those typical of bubonic plagues. For these reasons, some researchers are now proposing other diseases as the cause, such as pulmonary anthrax or the Ebola virus.

Q4 - Practice 3

The lecture discusses the rewriting of the history of the Great Zimbabwe civilization during the British Colonial period. The reading details the conclusions based on archaeological evidence. This evidence points to native Shona-speaking Africans as the founders of the civilization that boasted cities, royalty, and a monumental wall. British officials, on the other hand, put forth an official view that the civilization must have been built by foreigners from the north. Their hired archaeologists destroyed evidence and supported racist theories to justify imperialist ventures. Finally, after Zimbabwe gained its independence from Britain in 1980, the myth was dispelled and the truth became accepted.

Skill **C** Integrated Speaking: Stating Opinions and Summarizing

Necessary Skills

- Understanding the key information in listening passages
- Taking notes on important information and using this information in your spoken response
- Paraphrasing information
- Expressing an opinion or preference
- Supporting an opinion with reasons or examples

Strategies

- An organizational process for preparing your speech is detailed below. In each step, there are certain things that you need to keep in mind.

Process	Strategy
Listen to a conversation or a lecture	Take notes on the points and important details.
Read the question and understand the task	Identify what you will need to discuss.
Organize the ideas	Decide on your topic sentence and the supporting details. Be sure to include reasons and examples for any personal opinions expressed.

Skill C Q5 Practice 1 — Conversation

Step 1

Listen to a conversation. As you listen, take notes on one person's problem and the solutions suggested by the other person.

Problem: _____

_____

Solution 1: _____

_____

Solution 2: _____

_____

frazzled (adj):
feeling stress

take off (v phrase):
to go away

monumental (adj):
very large and important

shot (n):
an attempt; a try

check out (v):
to borrow; to officially remove from a library

Step 2

Read the question. Write down your opinion.

The students discuss two possible solutions to the woman's problem. Describe the problem. Then state which of the two solutions you prefer and explain why.

Problem: _____

Best solution: _____

Reason 1: _____

Reason 2: _____

Now create your own response using words and expressions from Steps 1 and 2. Use the prompts below to help you.

The woman's problem is _____

_____. The man and the woman _____ two options. The first option

_____. The second option _____

_____. I think the _____ option _____. She _____

_____. Also, _____ , so _____

_____.

Step 4

🎧 **Listen to the sample responses and compare them with your response above. Make notes about the differences you hear.**

Notes

Step 5

Review the response you wrote in Step 3 and your notes in Step 4. Then close your book and give a response to the question below. Say the response slowly and clearly. Try to speak for at least 60 seconds.

> The students discuss two possible solutions to the woman's problem. Describe the problem. Then state which of the two solutions you prefer and explain why.

Skill C Q5 Practice 2 — Conversation

Step 1

🎧 **Listen to a conversation. As you listen, take notes on one person's problem and the solutions suggested by the other person.**

Problem: _____

_____

Solution 1: _____

_____

Solution 2: _____

_____

drive someone crazy (v phrase):
to make someone very upset

in jeopardy (adj phrase):
at risk; in danger

manipulative (adj):
tending toward using people for one's own selfish reasons

tough out (prep phrase):
to endure; to remain strong in a difficult situation

bicker (v):
to argue

Step 2

Read the question. Write down your opinion.

The students discuss two possible solutions to the woman's problem. Describe the problem. Then state which of the two solutions you prefer and explain why.

Problem: _____

Best solution: _____

Reason 1: _____

Reason 2: _____

Step 3

Now create your own response using words and expressions from Steps 1 and 2. Use the prompts below to help you.

The woman is unhappy _____.

The man admits _____, but he recommends

_____.

In my opinion, _____. For one thing, _____

_____. Also, _____

_____.

Step 4

🎧 Listen to the sample responses and compare them with your response above. Make notes about the differences you hear.

Step 5

Review the response you wrote in Step 3 and your notes in Step 4. Then close your book and give a response to the question below. Say the response slowly and clearly. Try to speak for at least 60 seconds.

> The students discuss two possible solutions to the woman's problem. Describe the problem. Then state which of the two solutions you prefer and explain why.

Skill C **Q5** Practice 3 — Conversation

Step 1

🎧 **Listen to a conversation. As you listen, take notes on one person's problem and the solutions suggested by the other person.**

Problem: _____

_____

Solution 1: _____

_____

Solution 2: _____

_____

> **dissect** *(v):*
> to cut open for the purpose of study
>
> **gross** *(adj):*
> disgusting; revolting
>
> **hold against** *(v phrase):*
> to think badly of someone because of some event; to resent
>
> **suck it up** *(v phrase):*
> to quietly endure a difficult situation
>
> **virtual** *(adj):*
> simulated on a computer

Step 2

Read the question. Write down your opinion.

> The students discuss two possible solutions to the man's problem. Describe the problem. Then state which of the two solutions you prefer and explain why.

Problem: _____

Best solution: _____

Reason 1: _____

Reason 2: _____

Step 3

Now create your own response using words and expressions from Steps 1 and 2. Use the prompts below to help you.

The man's biology class is _____

_____. The woman suggests that _____

and _____. The man expresses concern, though,

that _____. I believe the man should _____

_____. He will _____

_____.

Step 4

🎧 **Listen to the sample responses and compare them with your response above. Make notes about the differences you hear.**

Notes

Step 5

Review the response you wrote in Step 3 and your notes in Step 4. Then close your book and give a response to the question below. Say the response slowly and clearly. Try to speak for at least 60 seconds.

> The students discuss two possible solutions to the man's problem. Describe the problem.
> Then state which of the two solutions you prefer and explain why.

Skill C Q6 Practice 1 — Lecture

Step 1

🎧 **Listen to a lecture. Fill in the missing information in the notes.**

Falconry is: _____

Falconers must: a) _____

                  b) _____

Today, falconry is: _____

Historically, falconry was: _____

Nomadic people in the desert: _____

Falconry dates back to: _____

prey (n): an animal that is hunted
tame (v): to teach a wild animal to obey commands
custom (n): an accepted practice
ritual (n): a practice repeated and performed a specific way for religious purposes
context (n): the circumstances surrounding a situation
nomadic (adj): relating to people who constantly move, who have no fixed home
procure (v): to get
enlist (v): to get the help of; to recruit
subsistence (n): the act or state of surviving
assert (v): to claim strongly; to contend

Step 2

Read the speaking task related to the lecture you heard.

> Using points and examples from the lecture, explain the origins of falconry and how it is practiced today.

Now create your own response using words and expressions from Step 1. Use the prompts below to help you.

Falconry was originally _____.

Nomadic people _____.

Today, in contrast, _____.

Nonetheless, _____.

The falconer _____.

Listen to the sample response and compare it with your response above. Make notes about the differences you hear.

Review the response you wrote in Step 2 and your notes in Step 3. Then close your book and give a response to the question below. Say the response slowly and clearly. Try to speak for at least 60 seconds.

Using points and examples from the lecture, explain the origins of falconry and how it is practiced today.

Skill C Q6 Practice 2 — Lecture

Step 1

🎧 **Listen to a lecture. Fill in the missing information in the notes.**

An aura is _____

Example: _____

Common characteristics of migraines: — _____

— _____

— _____

— _____

Process of migraine: _____

→ _____

→ _____

Possible way to prevent migraines from occurring: _____

_____

migraine (n): a severe form of headache
vomit (v): to force material from the stomach up through the throat and mouth
can't stand (v phrase): to hate; to not be able to tolerate
episodically (adv): occurring occasionally, but in clusters or groups
blood vessel (n): a vein or artery; a tube in the body through which blood can flow
stimulant (n): a material or event that causes a reaction
contract (v): to become smaller; to squeeze
compound (v): to add to; to make stronger or more intense
compensate (v): to make up for a shortcoming; to attempt to fix a problem
trigger (v): to start; to set off

Step 2

Read the speaking task related to the lecture you heard.

> Using points and examples from the lecture, explain what migraines are and how they occur.

Now create your own response using words and expressions from Step 1. Use the prompts below to help you.

A migraine is a _____.

The migraine itself involves _____ and other symptoms, such as _____.

Doctors suspect a possible cause _____.

The brain then _____, which results in pain. Migraine sufferers should try

to identify _____.

Step 3

Listen to the sample response and compare it with your response above. Make notes about the differences you hear.

Notes

Step 4

Review the response you wrote in Step 2 and your notes in Step 3. Then close your book and give a response to the question below. Say the response slowly and clearly. Try to speak for at least 60 seconds.

Using points and examples from the lecture, explain what migraines are and how they occur.

Step 1

🎧 **Listen to a lecture. Fill in the missing information in the notes.**

Standard view of evolution: Species arise _____

Example: _____

Counter-evidence: Source: _____

Trend: Species _____ for long periods of time.

New species _____.

New theory: _____

— Large populations typically _____

— Change occurs in _____

— After the change, the new species might _____

_____

The new theory _____ the standard view.

imperceptible *(adj)*:
too small to be noticed
punctuated *(adj)*: occasionally interrupted
dilute *(v)*: to make weaker; to decrease the ratio of
peripheral *(adj)*: to the side; not part of the center
novel *(adj)*: new; different from past examples
take over *(v phrase)*: to become dominant; to seize control
exterminate *(v)*: to kill; to destroy
predecessor *(n)*: a person or thing that comes before
complement *(v)*: to work well with; to improve the situation in combination with

Step 2

Read the speaking task related to the lecture you heard.

> Using points and details from the lecture, explain Punctuated Equilibrium and its relation to the standard, gradualist view of evolution.

Now create your own response using words and expressions from Step 1. Use the prompts below to help you.

The professor explains _____.

One example presented is _____.

This example supports _____. However, _____.

Punctuated Equilibrium is _____. It holds that _____

_____. On the other hand, _____

_____. The professor points out that the two theories _____

_____.

Step 3

🎧 **Listen to the sample response and compare it with your response above. Make notes about the differences you hear.**

Notes

Step 4

Review the response you wrote in Step 2 and your notes in Step 3. Then close your book and give a response to the question below. Say the response slowly and clearly. Try to speak for at least 60 seconds.

Using points and details from the lecture, explain Punctuated Equilibrium and its relation to the standard, gradualist view of evolution.

Skill C Integrated Speaking: Stating Opinions and Summarizing

Q5 - Practice 1

Opinion 1:

The woman's problem is that she does not have her university library card, but she needs to check out some books. The man and the woman discuss two options. The first option is that she just use the public library. The second option is that she try to find someone whose card she can borrow. I think the first option is better. She can go to the public library immediately without wasting any time looking for help. Also, there is no guarantee she would find anyone willing to be imposed upon, so the second option may be a waste of time.

Opinion 2:

The woman's problem is that she does not have her university library card, but she needs to check out some books. The man and the woman discuss two options. The first option is that she just use the public library. The second option is that she try to find someone whose card she can borrow. I think the second option is better. She can probably find a friend in her dorm who is more than happy to help her. Also, the public library may not have the resources she needs, so it may be a waste of time to go there.

Q5 - Practice 2

Opinion 1:

The woman is unhappy living with a friend who eats the woman's food and refuses to clean. The man admits the woman could just stick with the situation for a short time longer, but he recommends that she talk to her roommate about the problem. In my opinion, the woman should follow the man's recommendation. For one thing, it is not fair for her to have to do all the cleaning and pay for the food her roommate consumes. Also, if the woman convinces her roommate to start helping out, they will both be happier because there won't be any resentment between them.

Opinion 2:

The woman is unhappy living with a friend who eats the woman's food and refuses to clean. The man admits the woman could just stick with the situation for a short time longer, but he recommends that she talk to her roommate about the problem. In my opinion, the woman should follow her instincts and continue to live with her friend without complaint. For one thing, petty concerns are not worth losing a friend over. Also, if the roommate were to get upset and move out, the woman would be stuck paying all of the rent herself.

Q5 - Practice 3

Opinion 1:

The man's biology class is going to dissect a pig, and he does not want to take part because he believes that dissecting pigs is unethical. The woman suggests that he refuse to take part in the dissection and ask his teacher for an alternative project. The man expresses concern, though, that the teacher might be annoyed with him and lower his grade because of it. I believe the man should stick to his convictions and not take part in activities that contravene his beliefs. He will feel better about himself, and protesting might result in change.

Opinion 2:

The man's biology class is going to dissect a pig, and he does not want to take part because he believes that dissecting pigs is unethical. The woman suggests that he refuse to take part in the dissection and ask his teacher for an alternative project. The man expresses concern, though, that the teacher might be annoyed with him and lower his grade because of it. I believe the man should dissect the pig and not risk getting a poor grade. He will only have dissect the pig once, but a poor grade will cause him problems in the future.

Q6 - Practice 1

Falconry was originally employed as a tool to help people hunt food. Nomadic people in the desert tamed falcons in order to help them hunt for a larger variety of foods than they could acquire by themselves. Today, in contrast, people aren't as desperate to meet subsistence requirements. Nonetheless, falconry is still practiced as a sport. The falconer is highly skilled and must not only tame the falcon, but also teach it to hunt without killing the prey.

Q6 - Practice 2

A migraine is a severe headache that may be preceded by an aura, a symptom that signals the sufferer to the onset of a migraine. The migraine itself involves a headache and other symptoms, such as vomiting or intolerance for light or noise. Doctors suspect a possible cause is that restricted blood flow to the brain causes oxygen levels in the brain to decrease. The brain then tries to compensate by expanding the arteries in the brain, which results in pain. Migraine sufferers should try to identify what triggers their migraine to prevent further attacks.

Q6 - Practice 3

The professor explains two theories of evolution: one related to gradual evolution and the other related to rapid evolution. One example presented is the evolution of horses from cat-sized mammals to their much larger modern stature. This example supports the theory of gradual evolution. However, evidence in the fossil record indicates that species often remain unchanged for long periods, and then new species arise quite suddenly. Punctuated Equilibrium is a new theory that explains this. It holds that large populations dilute new mutations. On the other hand, beneficial mutations spread quickly in peripheral subpopulations. The professor points out that the two theories complement rather than contradict each other.

Vocabulary Review

Vocabulary Review 1

Instructions: Choose the best word or phrase to complete each sentence.

1. Her archaeology professor acted as her _____. He guided her through the difficulties of her master's program and helped shape the woman she is today.
   - (A) gadget
   - (B) curriculum
   - (C) mentor
   - (D) hindrance

2. She always _____ coffee in the morning. Without it, she can't work properly.
   - (A) craves
   - (B) hinders
   - (C) negates
   - (D) heeds

3. He developed a lot of _____ during his semester abroad. Afterwards, his parents trusted him with more responsibilities.
   - (A) destiny
   - (B) disruption
   - (C) incertitude
   - (D) maturity

4. There was a lot of _____ as crowds of people tried to see the famous actor walking through the mall.
   - (A) stamina
   - (B) discipline
   - (C) counsel
   - (D) commotion

5. After the air conditioning broke down, the students found the heat very _____. They just couldn't concentrate on the exam questions.
   - (A) diverting
   - (B) distracting
   - (C) crucial
   - (D) erudite

6. Because the government decided to construct a new highway through this land, they've decided to _____ the football stadium to another site.
   - (A) relocate
   - (B) relay
   - (C) allay
   - (D) abhor

7. We have decided to _____ on buying a car until we can save more money.
   - (A) figure out
   - (B) hold off
   - (C) redirect
   - (D) implement

8. Deciding what _____ to focus on in university can be a difficult decision.
   - (A) freebie
   - (B) mentor
   - (C) perseverance
   - (D) discipline

Instructions: Choose the word or phrase closest in meaning to the underlined part.

9. The huge snowstorm has <u>impeded</u> the progress of construction on the new library tower.
   - (A) excelled
   - (B) hindered
   - (C) revered
   - (D) relocated

10. A page listing your references is an <u>essential</u> component of your paper, so make sure you format it correctly.
    - (A) crucial
    - (B) diverting
    - (C) spoiled
    - (D) domestic

11. My friend is so <u>skeptical</u>. She never believes people are telling the truth.
- (A) domestic
- (B) erudite
- (C) crucial
- (D) cynical

12. Because our physics professor is attending a conference, Tuesday's lab session will <u>start</u> at 10:00 instead of 9:00.
- (A) commence
- (B) abhor
- (C) negate
- (D) heed

13. Could you please <u>pass</u> this information on to Dr. McCafferty?
- (A) inaugurate
- (B) relay
- (C) hold off
- (D) redirect

14. In general, a person's level of <u>doubt</u> increases as he or she encounters new information.
- (A) discipline
- (B) counsel
- (C) cacophony
- (D) incertitude

15. They have a good idea for a business <u>venture</u>. I think they're going to be quite successful.
- (A) dyslexia
- (B) stamina
- (C) expertise
- (D) enterprise

Instructions: Write the missing words. Use the words below to fill in the blanks.

diverting	gadget	better off
dyslexia	perseverance	

One **(16)** _____ that has helped me with school work is my "reading pen." To begin, I have **(17)** _____, a learning disability that makes reading very difficult. The reading pen not only made reading possible, it also made it quite **(18)** _____ for me. Without it, I would have spent tedious hours reading my assignments and probably would have given up. With **(19)** _____ and my reading pen, however, I was able to excel in school. I have been much **(20)** _____ because of it.

Instructions: Match the words that are opposites.

21. hinder   (A) ignore

22. heed   (B) love

23. commence   (C) pitch in

24. recipient   (D) sender

25. abhor   (E) hold off

Instructions: Choose the best word or phrase to complete each sentence.

1. When the forces on an object are balanced, the object is in _____.
(A) collusion
(B) equilibrium
(C) collision
(D) incubation

2. Because of the snowstorm, there was a _____ in my flight time. I had to spend an extra night in Norway.
(A) corollary
(B) plateau
(C) culprit
(D) delay

3. He has been trying to improve his grades, but instead, they have remained _____. At least they haven't gotten worse.
(A) static
(B) oncoming
(C) parasitic
(D) virtual

4. Their hypothesis needs to be analyzed with more _____. Experts have raised several questions about it that need answering.
(A) ritual
(B) subsistence
(C) scrutiny
(D) speciation

5. Nomadic tribes still wander across the Himalayan _____ in search of food.
(A) plateaus
(B) ravages
(C) customs
(D) migraines

6. Health officials are worried that a new _____ could spread across the planet, infecting millions of people with a serious, flu-like illness.
(A) herder
(B) prey
(C) stimulant
(D) pandemic

7. She has devised a _____ approach to measuring changes in ocean temperatures. Nothing like it has ever been employed before.
(A) punctuated
(B) nomadic
(C) novel
(D) manipulative

8. You will find that I manage in a manner quite different from my _____. Nonetheless, I hope to maintain the standard of excellence they have set.
(A) predecessors
(B) migraines
(C) rituals
(D) ravages

Instructions: Choose the word or phrase closest in meaning to the underlined part.

9. The <u>famous</u> publisher, David Asper, will be speaking on campus next Saturday afternoon.
(A) renowned
(B) static
(C) parasitic
(D) subsequent

10. Hybrid automobiles use gas power to <u>work well with</u> electric power.
(A) dilute
(B) exterminate
(C) compensate
(D) complement

11. I find astrophysics difficult enough, but to <u>add to</u> the problem, my vision is getting worse. I'm going to need to get glasses in order to read what the professor writes on the whiteboard.

(A) contract
(B) compound
(C) assert
(D) enlist

12. Egyptians began constructing <u>large, important</u> structures thousands of years ago.

(A) frazzled
(B) parasitic
(C) monumental
(D) renowned

13. The problem, <u>basically</u>, is that American industry depends on oil imported from overseas.

(A) in a row
(B) in essence
(C) in charge
(D) in jeopardy

14. The local government has <u>officially hired</u> a group of investigators to help solve the city's traffic problems.

(A) commissioned
(B) plundered
(C) contradicted
(D) migrated

15. Since different continents have different <u>types</u> of flu viruses, it is important to be cautious when traveling overseas during winter.

(A) advents
(B) culprits
(C) customs
(D) strains

Instructions: Write the missing words. Use the words below to fill in the blanks.

| imperceptible | asserts | peripheral |
| exterminate | dilute | |

The traditional view of evolutionary theory **(16)** _____ that species develop slowly, in a series of small **(17)** _____ stages. Evidence from the fossil record, however, indicates that species often remain unchanged for long periods, and then new species arise quite suddenly. Punctuated Equilibrium explains that large populations **(18)** _____ new mutations. In contrast, small **(19)** _____ subpopulations occurring in new environments allow beneficial mutations to spread quickly. Furthermore, when new species evolve from this spread, they often **(20)** _____ older species.

Instructions: Choose the one word that does not belong.

21. static   equilibrium   pandemic   unchanging

22. thrive   undermine   plunder   exterminate

23. dispel   contradict   bicker   enlist

24. vomit   ravages   migraine   complement

25. endure   tough out   surrender   suck it up

Chapter 2

Making Speech Coherent

A response to the independent speaking question usually has these components:

- An introduction to the general topic of the response—usually 1 sentence, but this can be skipped
- A statement of your opinion—generally 1 sentence
- Your reasons (2) + examples/details to support them—1 or 2 sentences each

Within 60 seconds, the time given to you for your response, you should be able to say about 8 sentences. These sentences would be similar in length to the following: "I often take my guitar to parties and play music for my friends there."

Before Speaking:

- Choose an opinion that is easily supported
- Organize the flow of your response in your mind
- Make sure that you have adequate reasons and examples

When Speaking:

- Make a clear statement of your opinion on the given topic
- State clear reasons for your opinion
- Use concrete examples
- Use transitions to order the flow of your speech

Skill A

Q1 Practice 1 — Personal Experience

Step 1

Read and think about the question below.

> These days, the world is truly becoming smaller, allowing for greater communication between people from different countries. Describe how you have been able to communicate with someone from another country and how it has affected your life. Use specific details and examples to explain your answer.

The sentences below make up part of a response to the question above. Read the sentences, and underline any transitions you find.

(A) By now, we have become good friends, and we have both learned a lot.

(B) Every week, we chat for 30 minutes in English and 30 minutes in Chinese.

(C) Last year, I met a fellow language student on an Internet study forum when I was trying to practice for a Chinese class.

(D) Later, we developed a symbiotic relationship by helping each other practice our respective languages.

(E) Of course, among the things I've learned is the fact that Chinese culture is fascinating, and this experience has really broadened my view of the world.

(F) As it turned out, he was a Chinese student trying to practice English.

fellow (adj):
belonging to the same group or engaged in the same activity

forum (n):
a site at which people with similar interests can communicate

symbiotic (adj):
beneficial to both parties

respective (adj):
individually

broaden (v):
to make wider

Look at the sentences again. Think of the role of each sentence in the response. Put the sentences in the right order.

				B				

Do NOT look at the sentences in Step 1. Answer the following questions.

1. How did the speaker meet his new friend?

_____

2. What do they do together now?

_____

3. How did this experience affect the speaker?

_____

Using the short answers you wrote above, try to speak for 60 seconds explaining the speaker's response. Use the words and phrases below while you are speaking. Time yourself and record the time below.

last year	when	later	every week	by now	of course	as it turned out

Response 1:   Speaking time: _____ seconds

Now, listen to a sample response. How is this response different from yours? What parts of the response can you use in your own? Write down any useful expressions the sample uses.

Notes

_____

_____

_____

_____

Listen again and repeat after the tape, paying attention to pronunciation, intonation, and word stress.

Now write your own answers to these questions.

1. How have you communicated with someone from another country?

_____

2. Who was this person, and what was the nature of your correspondence?

_____

3. How has this experience affected you?

_____

Using the short answers you wrote above, give a spoken response to the prompt below. Try to incorporate additional parts of speech from Step 3, while also paying attention to your pronunciation and intonation. Record your time.

> These days, the world is truly becoming smaller, allowing for greater communication between people from different countries. Describe how you have been able to communicate with someone from another country and how it has affected your life. Use specific details and examples to explain your answer.

Response 2:   Speaking time: _____ seconds

Skill A Q1 Practice 2 — Personal Experience

Step 1

Read and think about the question below.

> Describe a technological innovation that you have witnessed in your lifetime. Discuss how this invention has changed the way you live.

The sentences below make up part of a response to the question above. Read the sentences, underlining any transitions you find.

(A) After the Internet came into widespread use, however, I didn't have to go to the library at all.

(B) For example, I no longer had to make expensive, obligatory phone calls to my parents.

(C) One technological innovation I witnessed during my university days was the spread of the Internet.

(D) I could do all of my research from a computer in my dorm room, which saved a lot of time.

(E) Instead, I could send them updates via email for free.

(F) Before that, I spent hours in the library doing research.

(G) In fact, the Internet saved me a great deal of money, too!

widespread *(adj)*:
common in many places

obligatory *(adj)*:
done out of a sense of duty

innovation *(n)*:
a new and improved technology or way of doing something

witness *(v)*:
to see; to observe

update *(n)*:
information about new events in a person's life

Look at the sentences again. Think of the role of each sentence in the response. Put the sentences in the right order.

[ ] ▸ [ ] ▸ [A] ▸ [ ] ▸ [ ] ▸ [ ] ▸ [ ]

Do NOT look at the sentences in Step 1. Answer the following questions.

1. What was the speaker doing when Internet use became common?

_____

2. What is the first way the Internet changed the speaker's life?

_____

3. What is the second way the Internet changed the speaker's life?

_____

Using the short answers you wrote above, try to speak for 60 seconds explaining the speaker's response. Use the words and phrases below while you are speaking. Time yourself and record the time.

before that	for example	when	in fact	instead	which

Response 1:   Speaking time: _____ seconds

Step 3

🎧 **Now, listen to a sample response. How is this response different from yours? What parts of the response can you use in your own? Write down any useful expressions the sample uses.**

Notes

_____

_____

_____

_____

🎧 **Listen again and repeat after the tape, paying attention to pronunciation, intonation, and word stress.**

Now write your own answers to these questions.

1. What were you doing when some form of new technology became common?

_____

2. Name one way in which this form of technology has changed your life.

_____

3. Name another way in which this form of technology has changed your life.

_____

Using the short answers you wrote above, give a spoken response to the prompt below. Try to incorporate additional parts of speech from Step 3, while also paying attention to your pronunciation and intonation. Record your time.

> Describe a technological innovation that you have witnessed in your lifetime. Discuss how this invention has changed the way you live.

Response 2:   Speaking time: _____ seconds

Skill A **Q1** Practice 3 — Personal Experience

Step 1

Read and think about the question below.

> Unexpected weather can greatly affect our lives. Tell about a time when an unexpected storm or other weather event affected your life. Use specific details and examples to explain your answer.

A sample outline of a response is given below. Write down transition words or phrases that can be used in linking these ideas.

Unexpected weather event: snowstorm

- What happened: I was driving and I pulled over to help a stranded motorist.

- How it changed my life: I married the motorist.

Transition words:

_____   _____

_____   _____

_____   _____

Using this outline, give a spoken response to the prompt above. Time yourself and record the time.

Response 1:   Speaking time: _____ seconds

Step 2

Now, listen to a sample response. How is this response different from yours? What parts of the response can you use in your own? Write down any useful expressions the sample uses.

Notes

blizzard (n):
a severe snowstorm

raging (adj):
very strong and violent

stranded (adj):
stuck; unable to move or escape

pull over (v phrase):
to direct a moving vehicle to the side of a road and stop

lift (n):
a ride somewhere

Listen again and repeat after the tape, paying attention to pronunciation, intonation, and word stress.

Step 3

Now, give a spoken response to the prompt without listening to the sample. Try to incorporate additional parts of speech from Step 2, while also paying attention to your pronunciation and intonation. Record your time.

Response 2: Speaking time: _____ seconds

Step 4

Make up your own outline to the prompt. Try to incorporate transition words and useful phrases introduced earlier in the practice.

Unexpected weather event: _____

- What happened: _____
- How it changed my life: _____

Transition words:

_____ _____

_____ _____

_____ _____

Using this outline, give a spoken response to the prompt below. Time yourself and record the time.

> Unexpected weather can greatly affect our lives. Tell about a time when an unexpected storm or other weather event affected your life. Use specific details and examples to explain your answer.

Response 3: Speaking time: _____ seconds

Skill A Q1 Practice 4 — Personal Experience

Step 1

Read and think about the question below.

> Groups or organizations are an important part of some people's lives. Tell about a group or organization that is important to you. Use specific reasons and examples to explain your answer.

A sample outline of a response is given below. Write down transition words or phrases that can be used in linking these ideas.

Organization in my life — The Optimists' Club

- Reason 1 — organized activities for me

  Example — youth basketball league
- Reason 2 — helped me with problems

  Example — advice on school

Transition words:

_____ _____

_____ _____

_____ _____

Using this outline, give a response to the prompt above. Time yourself and record the time.

Response 1:   Speaking time: _____ seconds

Step 2

Now, listen to a sample response. How is this response different from yours? What parts of the response can you use in your own? Write down any useful expressions the sample uses.

Notes

optimist (n):
a person who always looks on the positive side of an event or experience

enriching (adj):
causing improvement; making better

forge (v):
to create; to establish

lasting (adj):
enduring; remaining strong for a long time

on edge (adj):
nervous; feeling great stress

Listen again and repeat after the tape, paying attention to pronunciation, intonation, and word stress.

Step 3

Now, give a spoken response to the prompt without listening to the sample. Try to incorporate additional parts of speech from Step 2, while also paying attention to your pronunciation and intonation. Record your time.

Response 2:   Speaking time: _____ seconds

Step 4

Make up your own outline to the prompt. Try to incorporate transition words and useful phrases introduced earlier in the practice.

Organization in my life — _____

- Reason 1 — _____
  Example — _____
- Reason 2 — _____
  Example — _____

Transition words:

_____   _____

_____   _____

_____   _____

Using this outline, give a response to the prompt below. Time yourself and record the time.

> Groups or organizations are an important part of some people's lives. Tell about a group or organization that is important to you. Use specific reasons and examples to explain your answer.

Response 3:   Speaking time: _____ seconds

Skill A Q2 Practice 1 — Personal Preference

Read and think about the question below.

> Do you agree or disagree with the following statement? The childhood years (the time from birth to twelve years of age) are the most important years of a person's life. Use specific reasons and examples to support your answer.

The sentences below make up part of a response to the question above. Read the sentences, and underline any transitions you find.

(A) Thus, it is crucial to have positive influences in childhood.

(B) Conversely, positive, nurturing experiences in childhood foster mental health and well-being in adulthood.

(C) For instance, a major trauma experienced at the age of six has a much more devastating effect than one experienced at age thirty.

(D) I believe that childhood is a critical period in a person's life.

(E) First, it is the time in which personality is developed.

(F) Second, a person's experiences in childhood affect the remainder of his or her life.

(G) Indeed, negative or traumatic experiences in childhood can lead to psychological problems in adulthood, such as depression and antisocial behavior.

remainder (n):
a part remaining; a part that is left

trauma (n):
an experience of great stress

antisocial (adj):
acting against society, i.e. criminal behavior

nurturing (adj):
caring and encouraging

foster (v):
to help develop

Look at the sentences again. Think of the role of each sentence in the response. Put the sentences in the right order.

| | > | | > | F | > | | > | | > | | > | |

Do NOT look at the sentences in Step 1. Answer the following questions.

1. What is the speaker's view of childhood?

_____

2. What is one reason the speaker gives for this view?

_____

3. What is a second reason the speaker gives for this view?

_____

Using the short answers you wrote above, try to speak for 60 seconds explaining the speaker's response. Use the words and phrases below while you are speaking. Time yourself and record the time.

first	second	for instance	so	clearly

Response 1:   Speaking time: _____ seconds

Step 3

🎧 Now, listen to a sample response. How is this response different from yours? What parts of the response can you use in your own? Write down any useful expressions the sample uses.

Notes

_____

_____

_____

🎧 Listen again and repeat after the tape, paying attention to pronunciation, intonation, and word stress.

Now write your own answers to these questions.

1. What is your view of the importance of childhood?

_____

2. What is one reason why you have this view?

_____

3. What is a second reason why you have this view?

_____

Using the short answers you wrote above, give a spoken response to the prompt below. Try to incorporate additional parts of speech from Step 3, while also paying attention to your pronunciation and intonation. Record your time.

> Do you agree or disagree with the following statement? The childhood years (the time from birth to twelve years of age) are the most important years of a person's life. Use specific reasons and examples to support your answer.

Response 2:   Speaking time: _____ seconds

Skill A Q2 Practice 2 — Personal Preference

Read and think about the question below.

> Some parents choose to home-school their children themselves rather than send them to public schools. In your opinion, which option is in the best interest of the child?

The sentences below make up part of a response to the question above. Read the sentences, underlining any transitions you find.

(A) These, I believe, are the most important skills learned at school.
(B) The skills I am referring to are social skills.
(C) Public schools, on the other hand, can and do provide this setting.
(D) Most parents are capable of teaching their children to read, write, add, and subtract, as well as many of the other basic skills children are taught at school.
(E) That's why I am of the opinion that children should learn in a social environment.
(F) However, there are some skills that cannot be taught sufficiently at home.
(G) Unfortunately, the home cannot provide an adequate social milieu for children to learn to live with a diverse group of people.

capable (adj):
able to do

sufficiently (adv):
well enough

adequate (adj):
sufficient; enough for a given purpose

diverse (adj):
many different

milieu (n):
a setting; an environment

Look at the sentences again. Think of the role of each sentence in the response. Put the sentences in the right order.

				E		

Do NOT look at the sentences in Step 1. Answer the following questions.

1. What does the speaker think parents can teach their children?

_____

2. What does the speaker think parents cannot adequately teach their children?

_____

3. Where does the speaker think children should be educated?

_____

Using the short answers you wrote above, try to speak for 60 seconds explaining the speaker's response. Use the words and phrases below while you are speaking. Time yourself and record the time.

that's why	however	I am referring to	unfortunately	on the other hand	these

Response 1:   Speaking time: _____ seconds

Step 3

Now, listen to a sample response. How is this response different from yours? What parts of the response can you use in your own? Write down any useful expressions the sample uses.

Notes

_____
_____
_____
_____

Listen again and repeat after the tape, paying attention to pronunciation, intonation, and word stress.

Now write your own answers to these questions.

1. What do you think parents can teach children?

_____

2. What do you think parents cannot teach children?

_____

3. Where do you think children should be educated?

_____

Using the short answers you wrote above, give a spoken response to the prompt below. Try to incorporate additional parts of speech from Step 3, while also paying attention to your pronunciation and intonation. Record your time.

> Some parents choose to home-school their children themselves rather than send them to school. In your opinion, which option is in the best interest of the child?

Response 2:   Speaking time: _____ seconds

Skill A Q2 Practice 3 — Personal Preference

Step 1

Read and think about the question below.

> Do you agree or disagree with the following statement? A zoo has no useful purpose. Use specific reasons and examples to explain your answer.

A sample outline of a response is given below. Write down transition words or phrases that can be used in linking these ideas.

Possible purpose 1: educate visitors — useful? Yes

Possible purpose 2: provide entertainment — useful? Yes

Possible purpose 3: protect animals — useful? Yes

Transition words:

_____   _____

_____   _____

_____   _____

Using this outline, give a spoken response to the prompt above. Time yourself and record the time.

Response 1:   Speaking time: _____ seconds

Step 2

Now, listen to a sample response. How is this response different from yours? What parts of the response can you use in your own? Write down any useful expressions the sample uses.

Notes

_____

_____

_____

_____

_____

multitude (n):
a large number; several

indigenous (adj):
native; naturally occurring in

captivating (adj):
interesting; engrossing

venue (n):
a place for a specific purpose

endangered (adj):
threatened; facing possible extinction

Listen again and repeat after the tape, paying attention to pronunciation, intonation, and word stress.

Step 3

Now, give a spoken response to the prompt without listening to the sample. Try to incorporate additional parts of speech from Step 2, while also paying attention to your pronunciation and intonation. Record your time.

Response 2:   Speaking time: _____ seconds

Step 4

Make up your own outline to the prompt. Think of other reasons to support the importance or lack of importance of zoos. Try to incorporate transition words and useful phrases introduced earlier in the practice.

Possible purpose 1: _____ useful? _____

Possible purpose 2: _____ useful? _____

Possible purpose 3: _____ useful? _____

Transition words:

_____   _____

_____   _____

_____   _____

Using this outline, give a spoken response to the prompt below. Time yourself and record the time.

> Do you agree or disagree with the following statement? A zoo has no useful purpose. Use specific reasons and examples to explain your answer.

Response 3:   Speaking time: _____ seconds

Skill A Q2 Practice 4 — Personal Preference

Step 1

Read and think about the question below.

> In some countries voting is obligatory; that is to say, all citizens are required to vote by law. In other countries, voting is optional. Which system do you think is better for a society? Include details and examples in your explanation.

A sample outline of a response is given below. Write down transition words or phrases that can be used in linking these ideas.

Prefer system in which voting is: optional

a. public interest more relevant

b. freedom not to vote

c. less authoritarian

Transition words:

_____ _____

_____ _____

_____ _____

Using this outline, give a spoken response to the prompt above. Time yourself and record the time.

Response 1:   Speaking time: _____ seconds

Step 2

Now, listen to a sample response. How is this response different from yours? What parts of the response can you use in your own? Write down any useful expressions the sample uses.

Notes

_____

_____

_____

_____

_____

turnout (n):
the level of participation in an activity

sway (v):
to convince; to change the opinion of

refrain (v):
to stop; to hold back

take part (v phrase):
to participate; to do something with others

constituent (n):
a person living in an area or district served by a politician

Listen again and repeat after the tape, paying attention to pronunciation, intonation, and word stress.

Step 3

Now, give a spoken response to the prompt without listening to the sample. Try to incorporate additional parts of speech from Step 2, while also paying attention to your pronunciation and intonation. Record your time.

Response 2:   Speaking time: _____ seconds

Step 4

Make up your own outline to the prompt. Think of other possible positive and negative factors for your choice. Try to incorporate transition words and useful phrases introduced earlier in the practice.

Prefer system in which voting is: _____

a. _____

b. _____

c. _____

Transition words:

_____   _____

_____   _____

_____   _____

Using this outline, give a spoken response to the prompt below. Time yourself and record the time.

> In some countries voting is obligatory; that is to say, all citizens are required to vote by law. In other countries, voting is optional. Which system do you think is better for a society? Include details and examples in your explanation.

Response 3:   Speaking time: _____ seconds

Skill A Independent Speaking: Test Questions 1 and 2

Q1 - Practice 1

Last year, I met a fellow language student on an Internet study forum when I was trying to practice for a Chinese class. As it turned out, he was a Chinese student trying to practice English. Later, we developed a symbiotic relationship by helping each other practice our respective languages. Every week, we chat for 30 minutes in English and 30 minutes in Chinese. By now, we have become good friends, and we have both learned a lot. Of course, among the things I've learned is the fact that Chinese culture is fascinating, and this experience has really broadened my view of the world.

Q1 - Practice 2

One technological innovation I witnessed during my university days was the spread of the Internet. Before that, I spent hours in the library doing research. After the Internet came into widespread use, however, I didn't have to go to the library at all. I could do all of my research from a computer in my dorm room, which saved a lot of time. In fact, the Internet saved me a great deal of money, too! For example, I no longer had to make expensive, obligatory phone calls to my parents. Instead, I could send them updates via email for free.

Q1 - Practice 3

My life was changed by an unexpected blizzard. One day when I left my house to go to the airport, the weather was cool but clear. As I was driving to the airport, though, it started snowing. Within minutes, there was a raging blizzard. I knew my flight to Jamaica was going to be canceled, so I was terribly disappointed. Then, I noticed a stranded motorist, so I pulled over to help. I offered the man a lift so he could call a tow truck. Three years later, I married that man. If it weren't for that blizzard, we wouldn't have met.

Q1 - Practice 4

The Optimists' Club is an organization that has been very important in my life. They organize fun and enriching activities for kids in the city. For example, I had a great experience and forged lasting friendships while participating in their youth basketball league. In addition, they provide counselors who help troubled youths with problems. One time, I was on edge about my high school course work, and I did not have anyone to turn to for guidance. The Optimists' Club counselor provided me with some very useful advice I needed in order to select the appropriate classes to enroll in.

Q2 - Practice 1

I believe that childhood is a critical period in a person's life. First, it is the time in which personality is developed. Second, a person's experiences in childhood affect the remainder of his or her life. For instance, a major trauma experienced at the age of six has a much more devastating effect than one experienced at age thirty. Indeed, negative or traumatic experiences in childhood can lead to psychological problems in adulthood, such as depression and antisocial behavior. Conversely, positive, nurturing experiences in childhood foster mental health and well-being in adulthood. Thus, it is crucial to have positive influences in childhood.

Q2 - Practice 2

Most parents are capable of teaching their children to read, write, add, and subtract, as well as many of the other basic skills children are taught at school. However, there are some skills that cannot be taught sufficiently at home. The skills I am referring to are social skills. These, I believe, are the most important skills learned at school. That's why I am of the opinion that children should learn in a social environment. Unfortunately, the home cannot provide an adequate social milieu for children to learn to live with a diverse group of people. Public schools, on the other hand, can and do provide this setting.

Q2 - Practice 3

I believe zoos serve a multitude of useful purposes. For one thing, zoos educate visitors. If there were no zoos, children would grow up never witnessing species not indigenous to their area. With zoos, in contrast, children can learn about all kinds of different animal species and observe them up close. That's more captivating and educational than looking at pictures or reading texts. For that matter, zoos provide an entertainment venue for people of all ages. Additionally, they provide a safe home for animals whose survival is threatened in the wild. Animals that are endangered can be kept safe and well fed, as well as be encouraged to breed.

Q2 - Practice 4

In some countries, all citizens are required to vote, while in others, individuals are free to decide whether to vote or not. I prefer the system in which voting is optional. First, in this system, public interest is more important because it affects voter turnout. Therefore, governments and candidates for office must work harder to sway the opinions of voters. Second, people should be free to protest an election by refraining from taking part. Indeed, the very idea of forcing constituents to vote runs counter to the principles upon which free society is based.

Responses for the integrated speaking generally include the following parts:

Question 3

- A statement of the problem or situation, as expressed in the reading
- A statement of the speaker's opinion, as introduced in the conversation
- His or her reasons + additional information, as taken from the conversation

Question 4

- A statement of the main idea or topic of the reading and lecture
- Key points that are similar
- Key points that contrast

Before Speaking:

- Identify the topic and supporting details
- Organize the flow of your response in your mind
- Make sure that you have adequate reasons and examples

While Speaking:

- Begin your response by clearly stating the opinion/main idea of the reading and the conversation/lecture
- Give reasons or details from the conversation or lecture to support your opinion
- Make sure statements are clearly connected so that the scorer will more easily understand your points

Skill B Q3 Practice 1 — Reading and Conversation

Step 1

Read the passage below and underline important information.

STUDY ABROAD PROGRAM NOTICE

Trinity is pleased to announce that we are currently accepting applications for next year's Study Abroad Program. In the past three years, we have organized successful exchanges in over thirty-five different countries on every continent with the exception of Antarctica. This is an invaluable opportunity for students to gain exposure to another culture while receiving academic credit. Students with need-based scholarships will be permitted to use their grant money toward tuition abroad. The cost of a semester abroad is normally comparable to tuition here at Trinity, though some exceptions do apply. The rewards afforded by this opportunity, however, are unparalleled.

invaluable (adj):
excellent

grant (n):
a sum of money given to students to pay for tuition

comparable (adj):
similar; approximately the same

afford (v):
to produce; to create

unparalleled (adj):
not equaled by others; the best

Write down the main idea and any important key points.

Notes

🎧 **Now listen to a related conversation. Take notes on the man's opinion.**

The problem: _____

Man's opinion of policy: _____

• Reason 1: _____

• Reason 2: _____

arbitrary (adj):
chosen or created without justification

technically (adv):
according to exact rules or definitions

fathom (v):
to understand; to comprehend

preclude (v):
to prevent; to forbid

merit (n):
a quality deserving praise or respect

Read and think about the prompt below.

> The man expresses his opinion of the policy regarding use of scholarships to pay for the study abroad program. State his opinion and explain the reasons he gives for holding that opinion.

WITHOUT looking at the original reading passage, review your notes from the reading and listening passages. Select the information you think is important. Fill in the blanks in the sample response below.

The man's opinion is that the school's policy _____

_____. To begin, _____

_____. Secondly, _____

_____. For these two reasons, he feels the woman _____

_____.

After you have filled in the blanks, read the response out loud. Pay attention to your pronunciation, intonation, and word stress. Record your time.

Response 1:   Speaking time: _____ seconds

Step 3

🎧 Now listen to a sample response. How does it differ from your response? Write down any differences in information or phrasing.

Notes

🎧 Listen again and repeat after the tape, paying attention to pronunciation, intonation, and word stress.

Step 4

Now, give your own spoken response to the prompt. Try to incorporate additional parts of speech from Steps 1 and 3, while also paying attention to your pronunciation and intonation. Record your time.

Response 2:   Speaking time: _____ seconds

Skill B Q3 Practice 2 — Reading and Conversation

Read the passage below and underline important information.

ANNOUNCEMENT: GRADUATE STUDENT HOUSING

We regret to inform all incoming first-year graduate students that due to renovations in the GS303 building, on-campus housing will be under limited availability during the upcoming academic year. All students are requested to sign up for the housing lottery by September 4th at www.dsu/administration/housing/lottery.htm. Arts and Humanities students as well as students in the Kurt Vonnegut Creative Writing Program will be given precedence. Students in the W. E. B. Dubois Sociology Program can sign up on the waiting list for housing in the undergraduate dorms. Partial tuition refunds will be proffered to students who do not receive a room assignment.

renovation (n):
a change to a room or building, usually for improvement

humanities (n):
the areas of study including literature, philosophy, and religion

precedence (n):
the opportunity to choose first; priority

partial (adj):
incomplete; in part

proffer (v):
to provide; to offer for acceptance

Write down the main idea and any important key points.

Notes

🎧 Now listen to a related conversation. Take notes on the woman's opinion.

Woman's opinion:

— lottery system is _____

Why:

— gives _____ but should be based on _____

— will cost her _____

— she won't be able to _____

What university should have done:

— _____

get by (v phrase):
to survive; to subsist

preferential (adj):
better; given more importance than others

prestige (n):
a level of high respect

pull in (v phrase):
to earn; to garner

give someone a piece of one's mind (expression):
to complain; to express anger

Read and think about the prompt below.

> The woman expresses her opinion of the announced plan. State her opinion and explain the reasons she gives for holding that opinion.

WITHOUT looking at the original reading passage, review your notes from the reading and listening passages. Select the information you think is important. Fill in the blanks in the sample response below.

The woman is angry about _____.

First, she thinks it is _____.

Instead, she believes _____.

Second, she is upset because _____.

For example, she will pay more _____.

In the end, she _____.

After you have filled in the blanks, read the response out loud. Pay attention to your pronunciation, intonation, and word stress. Record your time.

Response 1:   Speaking time: _____ seconds

Step 3

🎧 Now listen to a sample response. How does it differ from your response? Write down any differences in information or phrasing.

Notes

🎧 Listen again and repeat after the tape, paying attention to pronunciation, intonation, and word stress.

Step 4

Now, make your own spoken response to the prompt. Try to incorporate additional parts of speech from Steps 1 and 3, while also paying attention to your pronunciation and intonation. Record your time.

Response 2:   Speaking time: _____ seconds

Skill B Q4 Practice 1 — Reading and Lecture

Step 1

Read the passage below and underline the important information.

MARINE BIOLOGY: FEEDING PATTERNS

When studying the feeding patterns of sea life, marine biologists classify animals into two categories: active and passive. An active feeder, such as a shark, hunts for food aggressively. In contrast, a passive animal, such as a jellyfish, simply drifts, letting its food come to it. Marine biologists can make inferences about an animal's feeding behavior based on the morphology of its body. For example, passive feeders are characterized by mechanisms that allow them to catch prey, such as net-like organs to entangle smaller organisms. Active animals, conversely, typically have sharp teeth or some form of claw-like appendage.

drift *(v)*:
to move with the current of air or water

morphology *(n)*:
a design or shape

mechanism *(n)*:
a tool; a technique

entangle *(v)*:
to capture as with a net; to twist together

appendage *(n)*:
an attachment to a body, such as an arm or leg

Write down the main idea and any important key points.

Notes

_____

_____

_____

_____

_____

Now listen to a related lecture. Fill in the missing information.

Morphology of giant squid:

length: _____

appendages: _____

suckers: _____

Theories on feeding behavior:

passive reason: _____

active reasons: i) _____

ii) _____

elusive *(adj)*:
difficult to find or capture

in vain *(adv phrase)*:
without success or purpose

glean *(v)*:
to learn

carcass *(n)*:
a dead body

specimen *(n)*:
an example for scientific study

paradigm *(n)*:
a model

Read and think about the prompt below.

> The professor describes the physical morphology of the giant squid. Explain how this is related to the classification of the animal's feeding habits as active or passive.

WITHOUT looking at the original reading passage, review your notes from the reading and listening passages. Select the information you think is important. Fill in the blanks with this information in the sample response below.

The reading passage describes _____ .

The lecturer examines _____ .

First, the giant squid is _____ .

Second, it has _____ .

Some scientists have postulated that the _____ .

Other scientists, in contrast, point to _____ .

After you have filled in the blanks, read the response out loud. Pay attention to your pronunciation, intonation, and word stress. Record your time.

Response 1:   Speaking time: _____ seconds

Step 3

Now listen to a sample response. How does it differ from your response? Write down any differences in information or phrasing.

Notes

Listen again and repeat after the tape, paying attention to pronunciation, intonation, and word stress.

Step 4

Now, give your own spoken response to the prompt. Try to incorporate additional parts of speech from Steps 1 and 3, while also paying attention to your pronunciation and intonation. Record your time.

Response 2:   Speaking time: _____ seconds

Skill B Q4 Practice 2 — Reading and Lecture

Read the passage below and underline the important information.

MELODY AND SCALES

Historical records note that traditional European music was governed by three complementary concepts: rhythm, melody, and harmony. The most important concept, melody, deals with the order of the musical notes. Musicians discovered that certain patterns of notes sound like they belong together. As a consequence, these patterns became the standard for composing music.

These melody patterns are called scales. The two most important scales are the major and minor scales. The major scale is used to express cheer and triumph, while the minor scale is used to express mystery and enchantment. These two scales have been widely used throughout history to convey a range of human emotions.

govern (v):
to control; to make rules for

complementary (adj):
working well together

triumph (n):
a feeling of victory or celebration

enchantment (n):
a feeling of something strange and intriguing

convey (v):
to express; to communicate

Write down the main idea and any important key points.

Notes

_____

_____

_____

_____

Now listen to a related lecture. Fill in the missing information.

Early 20ᵗʰ Century: _____

— reaction to _____

— music fans _____

— composers _____

Atonal music

— used _____ scale

— contained _____ notes

uproar (n):
a state of shock and loud disagreement

plug (v):
to fill a hole in order to stop anything flowing through it

mutter (v):
to speak quietly and unhappily

lambaste (v):
to criticize harshly

uncouth (adj):
crude; unrefined; not sophisticated

go out the window (expression):
to become irrelevant; to not be used

Read and think about the prompt below.

The professor describes the beginnings of atonal music. Explain how this is related to the description of traditional music in the passage.

WITHOUT looking at the original reading passage, review your notes from the reading and listening passages. Select the information you think is important. Fill in the blanks with this information in the sample response below.

The professor begins by describing _____.

Listeners found the new style _____.

As the reading passage describes, traditional _____.

This music _____.

As the professor points out, atonal compositions _____.

The chromatic scale _____.

After you have filled in the blanks, read the response out loud. Pay attention to your pronunciation, intonation, and word stress. Record your time.

Response 1:   Speaking time: _____ seconds

Step 3

🎧 Now listen to a sample response. How does it differ from your response? Write down any differences in information or phrasing.

Notes

Step 4

Now, give your own response to the prompt. Try to incorporate additional parts of speech from Steps 1 and 3, while also paying attention to your pronunciation and intonation. Record your time.

Response 2:   Speaking time: _____ seconds

Skill B Integrated Speaking: Test Questions 3 and 4

Q3 - Practice 1

The man's opinion is that the school's policy of only allowing students with need-based scholarships to use that money toward the Study Abroad Program is unfair. To begin, he contends that the woman earned her scholarship through academic merit rather than athletic skill or financial need. Secondly, the woman did qualify for a need-based scholarship but opted for the academic one, showing that she has the same financial need as students with need-based scholarships. For these two reasons, he feels the woman should be allowed to use her grant money to pay for tuition abroad.

Q3 - Practice 2

The woman is angry about the announced plan for a housing lottery for graduate students. First, she thinks it is unfair because students of certain majors are being given priority. Instead, she believes the housing should be assigned based on need. Second, she is upset because living off campus will be expensive and inconvenient. For example, she will pay more in rent and transportation and will not be able to study late on campus. In the end, she complains that they should have done the renovations during the summer or otherwise accommodated the needs of all students.

Q4 - Practice 1

The reading passage describes the morphological differences between marine animals that are active feeders and passive feeders. The lecturer examines the morphology of the giant squid and different theories about its feeding habits. First, the giant squid is a very large creature. Second, it has two tentacles that include sharp, claw-like components. Some scientists have postulated that the enormous size of the giant squid suggests it must be a passive feeder. Other scientists, in contrast, point to its tentacles and the model of smaller squid species as evidence suggesting that the giant squid is an active feeder.

Q4 - Practice 2

The professor begins by describing the negative response many early-20th-century audiences had to the advent of atonal musical forms. Listeners found the new style too unstructured in comparison to the traditional forms they were used to. As the reading passage describes, traditional European music was based on principles of melody. This music utilized the major and minor scales to produce the desired emotions. As the professor points out, atonal compositions utilized the chromatic scale rather than the major or minor scales. The chromatic scale includes 12 notes, all the notes a person can play on the piano.

Responses for the integrated speaking generally include the following parts:

- A statement of the problem or situation, as expressed in the conversation
- A statement of suggested solutions, as mentioned in the conversation
- Your opinion of these suggested solutions
- Your reasons + examples and details to support them
- A summary of the main points of the lecture

Before Speaking:

- Choose an opinion most easily supported
- Organize the flow of your talk in your mind
- Make sure that you have adequate reasons and examples

When Speaking:

- Make a clear statement of your opinion on the given topic
- State clear reasons for your opinion
- Use concrete examples
- Use transitions to indicate the flow of your speech

To Describe Problems:

- She/He is having a problem with _____.
- The problem is _____.
- She/He needs help with _____.
- She/He is having trouble _____.
- She/He can't figure out _____.

To Present Opinions/Solutions:

- She/He needs to _____.
- She/He should _____.
- One (Another) thing she/he can do is _____.
- The best thing she/he can do is _____.
- If I were her/him, I'd _____.

Skill C Q5 Practice 1 — Conversation

Step 1

🎧 Listen to a conversation. Take notes on the problem presented and the possible solutions suggested.

Problem: _____

Solution 1: _____

    Advantages: _____

    Disadvantages: _____

Solution 2: _____

    Advantages: _____

    Disadvantages: _____

glitch (n):
a problem; an error

scanner (n):
a machine that reads the code on a card for information

find out (v phrase):
to discover; to learn

come through (v phrase):
to arrive

in training (adj phrase):
involved in a regiment of exercise; preparing for an athletic event

pain in the neck (expression):
an inconvenience; a nuisance

varsity (n):
a team representing a university or college

On your own, think of two or three additional possible benefits to each of the solutions suggested in the conversation. Write them in the spaces provided above.

Step 2

Read and think about the prompt below. Answer the following questions.

> The speakers discuss two possible solutions to the student's problem. Describe the problem. Then state which of the two solutions you prefer and explain why.

1. What is the problem? _____

2. What should the man do? _____

3. Why? _____

Step 3

Now create your own response to this topic using words and expressions from Steps 1 and 2. Use the prompts below to help you.

The man's problem _____ because _____ .

The woman suggests two solutions to his problem. First, _____ .

Second, _____ . In my opinion, the _____

choice is preferable. To begin, _____ .

In addition, _____ .

Now listen to a sample response. How does it differ from your response? Write down any differences in information or phrasing.

Notes

Listen again and repeat after the tape, paying attention to pronunciation, intonation, and word stress.

Step 4

Now, give your own spoken response to the prompt. Try to incorporate additional parts of speech from Step 3, while also paying attention to your pronunciation and intonation. Record your time.

Response: Speaking time: _____ seconds

Skill C Q5 Practice 2 — Conversation

Step 1

🎧 Listen to a conversation. Take notes on the problem presented and the possible solutions suggested.

Problem: _____

Solution 1: _____

     Advantages: _____

     Disadvantages: _____

Solution 2: _____

     Advantages: _____

     Disadvantages: _____

catch up *(v phrase)*:
to work fast enough to attain the same level as others

put one's nose to the grindstone *(expression)*:
to work very hard

from here on out *(adv phrase)*:
starting now and continuing until the end; from now on

pull off *(v phrase)*:
to do; to accomplish

extension *(n)*:
a delay in the date on which an assignment is due

dock *(v)*:
to subtract; to remove

suit *(v)*:
to please; to act according to preference

give something a shot *(expression)*:
to try; to make an attempt

heavy *(adj)*:
very serious; emotionally important

ASAP *(acronym)*:
as soon as possible

On your own, think of two or three additional possible benefits to each of the solutions suggested in the conversation. Write them in the spaces provided above.

Step 2

Read and think about the prompt below. Answer the following questions.

> The student has two possible choices in his current situation. Describe the situation. Then state which of the two choices you think is best and explain why.

1. What is the problem? _____

2. What should the man do? _____

3. Why? _____

Step 3

Now create your own response to this topic using words and expressions from Steps 1 and 2. Use the prompts below to help you.

The man's problem is that he wants _____ because

_____. In addition, _____.

The professor tries to _____.

In my opinion, he would be better off _____.

Even though he will _____, he will

_____.

🎧 **Now listen to a sample response. How does it differ from your response? Write down any differences in information or phrasing.**

Notes

🎧 **Listen again and repeat after the tape, paying attention to pronunciation, intonation, and word stress.**

Step 4

Now, give your own spoken response to the prompt. Try to incorporate additional parts of speech from Step 3, while also paying attention to your pronunciation and intonation. Record your time.

Response: Speaking time: _____ seconds

Skill C Q6 Practice 1 — Lecture

Step 1

Listen to a lecture. Take notes on the information presented.

Main topic of lecture: _____

    Origins of jazz and blues: _____

    _____

    Initial reactions: _____

    _____

    When became accepted: _____

    _____

    New forms today: _____

    _____

incarnation (n):
a new form of a familiar idea

norm (n):
a standard, or acceptable, behavior

mainstream (adj):
accepted by the majority

intoxicating (adj):
very fun and interesting; captivating

universally (adv):
by all people around the world

infancy (n):
the early years of; the period at the beginning

on the scene (adv phrase):
within a certain sphere of activity

sample (n):
an audio segment taken from an original piece and inserted, often repetitively, in a new recording

fusion (n):
a mixture

myriad (n):
a large number of different things

Step 2

Read and think about the prompt below. Answer the following questions.

> Summarize what you heard. Using points and examples from the talk, explain the development and innovations in music over the past one hundred years.

1. What development had the most influence on modern popular music?

_____

2. What changes did it bring to popular music?

_____

3. How did this music become accepted?

_____

Now create your own response to this topic using words and expressions from Steps 1 and 2. Use the prompts below to help you.

According to the lecture, the advent of _____ had a significant influence

_____. To begin, it was developed _____

_____. In addition, _____

influenced the development of _____.

At first, these musical forms _____.

Later, however, they became _____.

Furthermore, _____.

Now listen to a sample response. How does it differ from your response? Write down any differences in information or phrasing.

Notes

Listen again and repeat after the tape, paying attention to pronunciation, intonation, and word stress.

Step 4

Now, give your own spoken response to the prompt. Try to incorporate additional parts of speech from Step 3, while also paying attention to your pronunciation and intonation. Record your time.

Response: Speaking time: _____ seconds

Skill C Q6 Practice 2 — Lecture

Step 1

🎧 Listen to a lecture. Take notes on the information presented.

Main topic of lecture: _____

    Traditional conception of family: _____

    _____

    Those outside this conception: _____

    _____

    Today's families: _____

    _____

    Universal aspects of family: _____

    _____

conjure (v): to call or bring to mind; to evoke

pinpoint (v): to define with exactness

regurgitate (v): to reproduce exactly, without question or analysis

confines (n): the limits; the scope

marginalize (v): to put into a lower or outside group

pathological (adj): relating to unhealthy behavior

dysfunctional (adj): with abnormal or impaired functioning

adhere (v): to stick; to conform

alarmist (n): a person who exaggerates possible dangers in order to worry others

notion (n): a belief; a conception

Step 2

Read and think about the prompt below. Answer the following questions.

> Summarize what you heard. Using points and examples from the talk, explain the traditional ideal of family, its current status in American society, and the role of the family in society.

1. What is the traditional conception of an ideal family?

_____

2. What happened to families in the past that differed from this ideal?

_____

3. What role does family serve in all societies?

_____

Step 3

Now create your own response to this topic using words and expressions from Steps 1 and 2. Use the prompts below to help you.

In this lecture, the professor examines _____.

The traditional ideal of _____.

Furthermore, _____ in the past.

These days, however, only _____.

In point of fact, the professor relates that _____.

Finally, the professor states that _____.

Now listen to a sample response. How does it differ from your response? Write down any differences in information or phrasing.

Notes

Listen again and repeat after the tape, paying attention to pronunciation, intonation, and word stress.

Step 4

Now, give your own spoken response to the prompt. Try to incorporate additional parts of speech from Step 3, while also paying attention to your pronunciation and intonation. Record your time.

Response: Speaking time: _____ seconds

Sample Responses

Skill C Integrated Speaking: Test Questions 5 and 6

Q5 - Practice 1

The man's problem is that he cannot access the gym to work out because his student loans have not come through to pay his tuition. The woman suggests two solutions to his problem. First, he could find a student with access to accompany him to the gym. Second, he could talk to his coach and try to get a temporary ID. In my opinion, the first choice is preferable. To begin, his coach is away, so the man would have to wait. In addition, having a friend to work out with could help him maintain his exercise regime.

Q5 - Practice 2

The man's problem is that he wants to drop the professor's class because he is too far behind to earn a high grade. In addition, the deadline for dropping classes without penalty has passed. The professor tries to convince him to remain in the class and work hard to increase his grade. In my opinion, he would be better off dropping the class. Even though he will be penalized for dropping the class the same as if he had failed it, he will benefit by being able to concentrate his efforts on the courses of his major.

Q6 - Practice 1

According to the lecture, the advent of jazz music had a significant influence on the trajectory of popular music over the past 100 years. To begin, it was developed by African Americans combining African rhythms with European melodies. In addition, jazz influenced the development of blues, which added an extra note to the major scale, thus creating the blues scale. At first, these musical forms were met with resistance. Later, however, they became widely accepted after being incorporated into rock 'n' roll music by white musicians such as Elvis Presley. Furthermore, they have influenced the form of more recent popular music styles, such as hip-hop.

Q6 - Practice 2

In this lecture, the professor examines the idea of family. The traditional ideal of the family includes a working father, a domestic mother, and two or three children all living together in one home. Furthermore, families that differed from this ideal were marginalized and considered flawed or unhealthy in the past. These days, however, only a minority of families conform to this ideal. In point of fact, the professor relates that the ideal defined a generation or two ago is only one step on an ever-evolving sequence of ideals. Finally, the professor states that in all societies, the family helps define what is normal and natural.

Vocabulary Review

Vocabulary Review 1

Instructions: Choose the best word or phrase to complete each sentence.

1. The shark and the lamprey have a _____ relationship. The lamprey keeps the shark's skin clean, and the shark provides the lamprey with food.
   - (A) fellow
   - (B) symbiotic
   - (C) respective
   - (D) widespread

2. In this country, a handshake is _____ when making a business agreement. Without it, the parties involved may not trust one another.
   - (A) stranded
   - (B) antisocial
   - (C) diverse
   - (D) obligatory

3. The school decided not to open because of the _____. Driving on the streets would have been too dangerous.
   - (A) blizzard
   - (B) forum
   - (C) optimist
   - (D) milieu

4. Most students find studying abroad for a year to be an _____ experience. I strongly recommend you try it.
   - (A) enriching
   - (B) endangered
   - (C) adequate
   - (D) indigenous

5. Moving to a different city can cause a lot of _____ for young children.
   - (A) innovation
   - (B) trauma
   - (C) remainder
   - (D) multitude

6. The _____ has changed for our meeting. Now, we're going to gather in Mac Hall room 201, not the library.
   - (A) update
   - (B) blizzard
   - (C) lift
   - (D) venue

7. They sampled a _____ range of foods on their travels and want to try some of their different recipes with us.
   - (A) diverse
   - (B) capable
   - (C) nurturing
   - (D) lasting

8. *Robinson Crusoe* is a novel about a man who gets _____ on a deserted island. He is stuck there for several years before getting rescued.
   - (A) broadened
   - (B) stranded
   - (C) obligatory
   - (D) captivating

9. Let's quit for the day. We can finish the _____ of this work in the morning.
   - (A) remainder
   - (B) optimist
   - (C) innovation
   - (D) forum

10. Childhood violence can lead to _____ behavior in adulthood. Therefore, it should be avoided at all costs.
   - (A) endangered
   - (B) adequate
   - (C) capable
   - (D) antisocial

11. The teacher demands that students
    _____ from chewing gum in class.
    (A) sway
    (B) refrain
    (C) fathom
    (D) proffer

12. The new law insists that government
    contracts be awarded on _____.
    Only the best proposals will be accepted,
    and no favoritism will be allowed.
    (A) merit
    (B) renovation
    (C) prestige
    (D) constituents

13. The professor's decision to give her an F
    seems completely _____! I can see
    no justification for it.
    (A) partial
    (B) preferential
    (C) unparalleled
    (D) arbitrary

14. The group from my university were able to
    _____ the opinion of the scientific
    community. Now, the validity of their theory
    is widely accepted.
    (A) sway
    (B) afford
    (C) complement
    (D) dilute

15. The _____ for the marathon for
    cancer research was higher than expected.
    Over 2,000 runners participated!
    (A) grant
    (B) humanities
    (C) turnout
    (D) prestige

Instructions: Choose the word or phrase closest
in meaning to the underlined part.

16. Her strongest friendships were <u>established</u> in
    high school.
    (A) broadened
    (B) proffered
    (C) forged
    (D) precluded

17. You seem to be <u>feeling a lot of stress</u> these
    days. Is there something I can help you with?
    (A) preferential
    (B) on edge
    (C) arbitrary
    (D) captivating

18. The encouragement of her parents <u>helped
    develop</u> her skill as an artist.
    (A) fostered
    (B) fathomed
    (C) witnessed
    (D) refrained

19. A grade of C will be <u>sufficient</u> to pass to the
    next level; however, higher grades could earn
    you scholarship money.
    (A) endangered
    (B) respective
    (C) exclusive of
    (D) adequate

20. The palm tree is not <u>native</u> to California. It was
    introduced to the area by Spanish settlers.
    (A) stranded
    (B) indigenous
    (C) invaluable
    (D) partial

21. The police questioned seven people who
    <u>observed</u> the bank robbery.
    (A) forged
    (B) precluded
    (C) compensated
    (D) witnessed

22. People can suffer from a <u>large number</u> of
    fears. My strongest fear is of heights.
    (A) remainder
    (B) renovation
    (C) constituent
    (D) multitude

23. Many species of amphibian are becoming
    <u>threatened</u>. If we do not take action to save
    them, they may become extinct.
    (A) adequate
    (B) endangered
    (C) invaluable
    (D) preferential

24. That is an <u>engrossing</u> film. I couldn't take my
    eyes away from the screen when I watched it.
    (A) captivating
    (B) nurturing
    (C) revolting
    (D) manipulative

25. A <u>strong and violent</u> storm shut down most
    of the cities along the coast.
    (A) partial
    (B) punctuated
    (C) raging
    (D) symbiotic

26. This project gets <u>priority</u> over that one. We
    should complete it first.
    (A) precedence
    (B) turnout
    (C) constituent
    (D) merit

27. The school on the east coast <u>provided</u> her an
    athletic scholarship, but she declined the offer
    and attended a school on the west coast
    instead.
    (A) pulled in
    (B) proffered
    (C) refrained
    (D) swayed

28. The view of the ocean from this house is <u>the
    best</u>. I think you should buy it.
    (A) exclusive of
    (B) arbitrary
    (C) imperceptible
    (D) unparalleled

29. His injured leg <u>prevented</u> him from competing
    in the Olympic games.
    (A) forged
    (B) afforded
    (C) precluded
    (D) fostered

30. Her parents could never <u>understand</u> her
    decision to relocate overseas.
    (A) fathom
    (B) broaden
    (C) exterminate
    (D) compound

Instructions: Write the missing words. Use the words below to fill in the blanks.

fellow	symbiotic	fostered	unparalleled	forged
diverse	indigenous	invaluable	swayed	milieu

While searching for information on fishing in the Northwest, I encountered a website run by a **(31)** _____ fishing enthusiast. As it turned out, he was a Korean student trying to practice English on his website. Later, we met and developed a **(32)** _____ relationship by helping each other. I **(33)** _____ his learning of English, while he showed me **(34)** _____ fishing spots in our area. Through these interactions, we have **(35)** _____ a strong friendship. Over the time we have known each other, he has introduced me to a **(36)** _____ range of places for fishing, and I have also tasted a large variety of fish **(37)** _____ to this region of the country. I consider our friendship to be **(38)** _____. In fact, my friend has **(39)** _____ me to join him on a fishing expedition down south. He loves traveling and finds the cultural and natural **(40)** _____ of the US to be captivating.

Instructions: Choose the one word which does not belong.

41. innovation   forum   venue   site

42. sufficient   adequate   capable   endangered

43. stressed   diverse   frazzled   on edge

44. refrain   preclude   afford   stop

45. invaluable   obligatory   unparalleled   monumental

Instructions: Label each pair of words as similar (S) or opposite (O).

46. _____ symbiotic   parasitic

47. _____ widespread   common

48. _____ optimist   cynic

49. _____ foster   nurture

50. _____ foreign   indigenous

Instructions: Choose the best word or phrase to complete each sentence.

1. An examination of the _____ of an animal's teeth can show if that animal is a predator.
   - (A) appendage
   - (B) carcass
   - (C) morphology
   - (D) triumph

2. She's been saving for a trip to Europe for three years. Unfortunately, reaching that goal is proving _____. She still needs a lot more money.
   - (A) elusive
   - (B) complementary
   - (C) uncouth
   - (D) mainstream

3. They celebrated in _____ after their country's team won the World Cup.
   - (A) extension
   - (B) incarnation
   - (C) fusion
   - (D) triumph

4. The cartoon mouse has gone through several different _____. The earliest drawings of him look much different from current ones.
   - (A) norms
   - (B) incarnations
   - (C) myriads
   - (D) confines

5. Societies all over the world have _____ individuals whose appearances differ from the norm. Slowly, however, many groups are trying to be more inclusive.
   - (A) marginalized
   - (B) conjured
   - (C) adhered
   - (D) suited

6. When my father was a young student, they were taught to memorize information and _____ it for exams. Thankfully, those teaching techniques have become outdated.
   - (A) pinpoint
   - (B) dock
   - (C) regurgitate
   - (D) catch up

7. The professor has given us all an _____ for the term papers. They're now due on Friday.
   - (A) incarnation
   - (B) extension
   - (C) infancy
   - (D) alarmist

8. The bottle _____ with the ocean current all the way to Japan.
   - (A) entangled
   - (B) drifted
   - (C) gleaned
   - (D) lambasted

9. Within the rainforest exist a _____ of plant and animal life forms.
   - (A) myriad
   - (B) notion
   - (C) scanner
   - (D) mechanism

10. The _____ of a dead great white shark washed up on shore last summer.
   - (A) carcass
   - (B) paradigm
   - (C) triumph
   - (D) enchantment

11. The fly _____ itself in the spider's web.

(A) gleaned
(B) entangled
(C) governed
(D) came through

12. If you don't want to take my advice, then _____ yourself. I think, however, that you will regret your decision.

(A) dock
(B) broaden
(C) suit
(D) witness

13. Because the team was _____ as a group, the management decided that a change in personnel was needed.

(A) intoxicating
(B) complementary
(C) mainstream
(D) dysfunctional

14. Ireland is famous for evoking pleasant feelings of mystery and _____ in its visitors.

(A) infancy
(B) extension
(C) morphology
(D) enchantment

15. Passionate Canadians everywhere were in a state of _____ upon learning of the cancellation of the hockey season.

(A) uproar
(B) appendage
(C) paradigm
(D) innovation

Instructions: Choose the word or phrase closest in meaning to the underlined part.

16. The Wright brothers set a <u>model</u> of powered aircraft that others would follow in the future.

(A) specimen
(B) paradigm
(C) glitch
(D) scanner

17. Many people find the <u>belief</u> that women should not have careers to be insulting and outdated.

(A) notion
(B) sample
(C) varsity
(D) uproar

18. Wolf behavior is <u>controlled</u> by the hierarchical structure of the pack.

(A) plugged
(B) muttered
(C) conveyed
(D) governed

19. There is some <u>error</u> with this program. It won't print what I want it to.

(A) myriad
(B) norm
(C) glitch
(D) varsity

20. Her boss <u>subtracted</u> fifty dollars from her pay every time she arrived for work late.

(A) conjured
(B) regurgitated
(C) suited
(D) docked

21. Due to recent events, professors are reminded that the <u>scope</u> of the teacher-student relationship does not allow for dating.
    (A) confines
    (B) fusion
    (C) infancy
    (D) extension

22. Unfortunately, we must <u>conform</u> to the company's rules for employee age. Therefore, your application has not been accepted.
    (A) pinpoint
    (B) adhere
    (C) marginalize
    (D) preclude

23. His mother believes that anyone who does not listen to Mozart on a daily basis is <u>uncivilized</u>.
    (A) preferential
    (B) unparalleled
    (C) endangered
    (D) uncouth

24. Darwin collected many <u>examples</u> of new plant and animal species for scientific examination.
    (A) specimens
    (B) carcasses
    (C) humanities
    (D) renovations

25. His wife <u>harshly criticized</u> him for arriving home from work at 1:00 a.m.
    (A) lambasted
    (B) pinpointed
    (C) broadened
    (D) forged

26. The <u>standards</u> of one culture may seem odd to people from another culture.
    (A) mentors
    (B) norms
    (C) stimulants
    (D) plateaus

27. The atmosphere at the festival was <u>exhilarating</u>. None of us wanted the day to end.
    (A) mainstream
    (B) intoxicating
    (C) peripheral
    (D) imperceptible

28. During its <u>early years</u>, the Internet was not used in most homes as it is today.
    (A) incarnation
    (B) varsity
    (C) morphology
    (D) infancy

29. The braking <u>tool</u> on my bicycle is broken, so I can't ride today.
    (A) appendage
    (B) mechanism
    (C) glitch
    (D) forum

30. The children <u>complain quietly</u> whenever their mother makes them study.
    (A) plug
    (B) convey
    (C) glean
    (D) mutter

Instructions: Write the missing words. Use the words below to fill in the blanks.

indigenous	elusive	myriad	in vain	specimens
lambaste	glean	convey	optimists	mainstream

The sasquatch, a large ape-like creature **(31)** _____ to North America has proven to be **(32)** _____. Over the past thirty years, a **(33)** _____ of expeditions have been launched in the attempt to capture a sasquatch. Unfortunately, these efforts have been **(34)** _____ as none have yet been captured. Because no actual **(35)** _____ have been captured for study, most scientists doubt its existence. Some go even so far as to **(36)** _____ colleagues who support the idea of its existence. Despite these cynical colleagues, researchers have discovered some evidence that helps science **(37)** _____ information about this mysterious animal. For example, sasquatch nests and droppings **(38)** _____ key details about its sleeping and eating habits. **(39)** _____ among the group of sasquatch researchers strongly believe the day will come when living examples of the animal will be discovered, and their theories will become accepted by **(40)** _____ science.

Instructions: Write the missing word. Use the words below to fill in the blanks.

off	by	in	in	over

41. If a police car turns on its sirens, you should pull _____ immediately.

42. We decided to take part _____ the protest against the war.

43. I depend on my student loans to get _____. Without them, I couldn't survive.

44. He tried _____ vain to find the information on the Internet. After three hours, he gave up and went to the library.

45. After a lot of hard work and constant study, she was able to pull _____ the highest grade in the class.

Instructions: Match the words that are opposites.

46. alarmist   (A) release

47. include   (B) marginalize

48. complementary   (C) forget

49. entangle   (D) optimist

50. glean   (E) dysfunctional

Chapter 3

Focus: Speaking Naturally

Focus A   Sentence Stress

- Sentence stress on content words
- Sentence stress on function words

Focus B   Stress and Intonation

- Changing pitch for emphasis
- Commas and series with *and* or *or*

Focus C   Pausing

- Timing
- Pause and pitch

Focus | Speaking Naturally

Using the tips below, you can improve both your fluency and clarity of speech. These tips will also help you recognize your weak points in speaking.

When speaking:
- Open your mouth while speaking. Try not to mumble.
- Pay special attention to the pronunciation of content words and key terms.
  - Stress each syllable correctly and accurately.
  - Clearly pronounce both vowels and consonants.
  - Smoothly link sounds between words within a phrase and in consonant clusters.
- Change pitch between stressed and unstressed syllables.
- Speak in sentences or phrases, not word by word.
- Speak with appropriate speed, not too quickly.

When practicing:
- Practice speaking by writing down every word you say and marking each place where you pause or vary intonation.
- Examine this transcript of your speech and look for possible mistakes. Practice these parts again, focusing on correcting the previous mistakes.
- Record and listen to your speech. Note any areas that need improvement.

Sentence stress is very important in English. The rhythm of sentences spoken in English alerts listeners to the message presented. Words or phrases important to the content of the message tend to be stressed, whereas words or phrases that are not important tend to be reduced.

Focus A - Sentence Stress

Step 1 Sentence stress on content words

Certain words within a sentence are given importance because of the meaning they communicate. These words are referred to as content words. Words with little or no meaning outside their grammatical function are usually not stressed within the sentence.

— Content Words: nouns, verbs, adjectives, adverbs

— Function Words: auxiliary verbs, *be* verbs, most pronouns, prepositions, articles

Stressed syllables are pronounced longer, pitched higher, and spoken slightly louder.

Underline the content words and say the sentence. Be sure to stress the content words.

1. Before that, I spent hours in the library doing research.
2. My life was changed by an unexpected blizzard.
3. In addition, they provide counselors who help troubled youths with problems.
4. I believe that childhood is an integral period in a person's life.
5. Public schools, on the other hand, can and do provide this setting.
6. That's more captivating and educational than looking at pictures or reading texts.
7. I prefer the system in which voting is optional.
8. Instead, she believes the housing should be assigned based on need.

Now, listen and repeat.

Listen to the paragraph. Write only the words you hear most clearly.

Step 2 Sentence stress on function words

> The normal pattern of sentence stress reduces function words. However, function words can be stressed when the speaker is expressing strong emotion, is disagreeing, or is clarifying mistaken information.
>
> Ex. <u>Don't</u> you agree that English is easy?
>
> I <u>do not</u> agree! (Non-contracted forms are often used to show stress.)

Say the sentences and indicate whether the underlined word is reduced (R) or stressed (S).

1. Technically, my scholarship isn't need-based, but I <u>do</u> need it.
2. If you put your nose to the grindstone from here on out, you <u>might</u> pull off a C.
3. After the Internet came along, I <u>could</u> do all of my research from a computer in my dorm room.
4. First, <u>it</u> is the time in which personality is developed.
5. However, there are some skills that <u>cannot</u> be taught sufficiently at home.
6. Public schools, on the other hand, <u>can</u> and <u>do</u> provide this setting.
7. In my opinion, the second choice <u>is</u> preferable.
8. Although no specimens have been found, there <u>is</u> a lot of evidence for scientists to examine.

Now, listen and repeat.

Circle any underlined words that should be stressed. More than one word may be stressed in each sentence.

Example. We didn't <u>have</u> a lot of rain last year, <u>but</u> we (do) this year.

1. That <u>isn't</u> <u>his</u> dog, <u>it's</u> <u>her</u> dog.
2. Most students <u>didn't</u> pass <u>the</u> exam, but John <u>did</u>.
3. She <u>likes</u> jazz music, <u>and</u> he likes blues music. I like jazz <u>and</u> blues music.
4. Kim <u>hasn't</u> paid <u>her</u> tuition fees, but Rick <u>has</u>.
5. The major scale <u>doesn't</u> have 12 notes, <u>but</u> the chromatic scale <u>does</u>.
6. Off-campus housing <u>isn't</u> just expensive; <u>it's</u> expensive <u>and</u> inconvenient.
7. <u>He</u> <u>didn't</u> get the need-based scholarship. <u>She</u> did.
8. You <u>can</u> take English 201 <u>or</u> English 205. You can't take both.

Now, listen and repeat.

Intonation is also very important in English. The pitch of the speaker's voice alerts listeners to the particular message being conveyed. By modifying the pitch of the voice to rise, fall, or do both, the speaker stresses certain words and meanings. When modifying the pitch, the speaker often lengthens the amount of time each word is pronounced.

Focus B - Stress and Intonation

Step 1 Changing pitch for emphasis

At the beginning of a conversation, the last content word in each sentence is usually the focus of meaning. Therefore, the primary stress in these sentences usually falls on the last content word. The sound of the speaker's voice rises on the focus word and then falls. If the sentence is a question, the sound of the speaker's voice rises but does not fall at the end of the sentence.

Ex. Is that a deer? No, it's a big dog.

However, the focus of a sentence can change. Thus, one sentence can have more than one intonation pattern. By noticing the word the speaker emphasizes, the listener can guess what will come next.

Ex. It's not a small dog. It's a big dog.

Listen to the first sentence and underline the focus word. Then choose the sentence that is most likely to come next.

1. Children should attend school.
   a. Adults should work.
   b. It's a good place to learn social skills.
2. This experience helped tremendously with my studies.
   a. I really learned a lot.
   b. Unfortunately, it didn't help with her studies.
3. Subsequent developments in pop music were generally met with the same disapproval.
   a. Hip-hop and reggae, for example, took a long time to reach the mainstream.
   b. Developments in classical music, on the other hand, were embraced in a short time.
4. Do you play on the varsity basketball team?
   a. No, I play on the hockey team.
   b. No, John plays on the basketball team.

Now, listen and repeat. Ensure your voice is rising on the stressed syllables and dropping afterwards.

Read the two sentences. Try to figure out how the second sentence relates to the first. Underline the focus word in the first sentence according to this context.

1. I don't abhor jazz music. I don't really enjoy it that much, though.
2. Her behavior is antisocial. He is actually a nice guy.
3. The squid doesn't have eight appendages. It has ten.
4. Jellyfish drift with ocean currents. Squid use their arms to swim.
5. There is a glitch with her computer. Her phone is working fine.
6. The campus renovations will begin in September. The campus celebrations begin in October.

Now, listen and repeat. Ensure your voice is rising on the stressed syllables and dropping afterwards.

Step 2 Commas and series with *and* or *or*

When there is a series of words with the conjunctions *and* or *or*, the intonation rises on all members of the series except the last. The last member has a rising-falling intonation.

Ex. We went to the park, / (↗) the beach, / (↗) and the mountains. (↘)

You can do it Monday / (↗) or Tuesday. (↘)

After the comma used between a sentence and an additional phrase, the intonation rises.

Ex. It's three blocks from here, / (↗) near the supermarket. (↘)

As for me, / (↗) I'll have the soup and salad. (↘)

Divide the sentences into thought groups by using slashes (/) and mark the intonation of each group with arrows (↗ or ↘).

1. Many of the most popular bands on the charts today are born from influences of rock, hip-hop, reggae, ska, and techno.
2. They were considered troubled, pathological, or dysfunctional.
3. I doubt it'll cover the cost of renting a place in this city, especially near the campus.
4. Most giant squid are smaller, growing to approximately ten meters.
5. European concert-goers were plugging their ears, walking out on performances, and muttering to themselves.
6. The chromatic scale simply means all the notes you can play on a piano, without any notes left out.

Now, listen and repeat.

Having appropriate pauses is also an important part of spoken English. Pauses are given after each message unit in order to provide listeners time to process the information. If a speaker speaks too rapidly or without thought to the grouping of the information presented, listeners may have difficulty distinguishing the important content of the message.

Focus C - Pausing

Step 1 Timing

Pausing, like stress and pronunciation, greatly adds to the clarity of speech.

There are several reasons for adding a pause:
- To make the meaning clear: When the wind blows [pause] the waves run high.
- For emphasis: Frankly [pause] I'm disappointed in you.
- To enable the speaker to catch a breath
- To give listeners time to understand complex sentences

Therefore, it is helpful to pause after commas, transitional words, and complicated ideas, such as lengthy subjects, prepositional phrases, and clauses in compound and complex sentences.

Look at the sentences and circle any slash (/) that indicates an appropriate pause.

1. The traditional ideal / of the family includes a working father, / a domestic mother, / and two or three children all living / happily in one home.
2. As it turned out, / he was a Chinese student / trying to practice English.
3. After the Internet / came into widespread use, / however, / I didn't have to go to the library at all.
4. Within minutes, / there was a raging / blizzard.
5. Some alarmists / contend that this is a fundamental societal problem, / a breakdown in values that will produce / immeasurable negative effects.
6. These, / I believe, / are the most important / skills learned at school.

Now, listen and repeat.

Practice saying the sample response and write a slash (/) where you pause.

1. The man's opinion is that the school's policy of only allowing students with need-based scholarships to use that money toward the Study Abroad Program is unfair.
2. To begin, he contends that the woman earned her scholarship through academic merit rather than athletic skill or financial need.
3. Secondly, the woman did qualify for a need-based scholarship but opted for the academic one, showing that she has the same financial need as students with need-based scholarships.
4. For these two reasons, he feels the woman should be allowed to use her grant money to pay for tuition abroad.

Now, listen and repeat.

Step 2 Pause and pitch

Every clause or thought group within a sentence contains a focus word. A rise and then a fall in pitch is used to mark this focus word. This change alerts listeners to the central meaning of the thought group. The fall in intonation, combined with pausing, helps listeners recognize the end of a thought group.

Ex. I remembered to bring paper, / but I forgot my book.
When the water boils rapidly, / put the spaghetti in the pot.
When the water boils, / rapidly put the spaghetti in the pot.

Practice saying the sentences. Be sure to use appropriate pauses and pitch.

1. The reading passage describes the morphological differences between marine animals that are active feeders and passive feeders.
2. The lecturer examines the morphology of the giant squid and different theories about its feeding habits.
3. First, the giant squid is a very large creature.
4. Second, it has two tentacles that include sharp, claw-like components.
5. Some scientists have postulated that the enormous size of the giant squid suggests it must be a passive feeder.
6. Other scientists, in contrast, point to its tentacles and the model of smaller squid species as evidence suggesting the giant squid is an active feeder.

Now, listen and repeat.

Practice Test

Practice Test

Section | Options | | | Directions | Testing Tools
Speaking | Pause | Section Exit | | Continue | Volume | Back | Next | Help

Speaking Section

Directions

In this section of the test, you will demonstrate your ability to speak about a variety of topics. You will answer six questions by speaking into the microphone. Answer each of the questions as completely as possible.

In questions one and two, you will speak about familiar topics. Your response will be scored on your ability to speak clearly and coherently about the topics.

In questions three and four, you will first read a short text. The text will go away and you will then listen to a talk on the same topic. You will be asked a question about what you have read and heard. You will need to combine appropriate information from the text and the talk to provide a complete answer to the question. Your response is scored on your ability to speak clearly and coherently and on your ability to accurately convey information about what you read and heard.

In questions five and six, you will listen to part of a conversation or a lecture. You will be asked a question about what you heard. Your response is scored on your ability to speak clearly and coherently and on your ability to accurately convey information about what you heard.

You may take notes while you read and while you listen to the conversations and lectures. You may use your notes to help prepare your responses.

Listen carefully to the directions for each question. The directions are not shown on the screen.

For each question, you will be given a short time to prepare your response. A clock will show how much preparation time is remaining. When the preparation time is up, you will be told to begin your response. A clock will show how much time is remaining. A message will appear on the screen when the response time has ended.

If you finish before the allotted time, press **Continue** to go to the next question.

Question 1

Section
Speaking

Question
1 of 6

Testing Tools

Volume | Back | Next | Help

Some people trust their first impressions about a person's character because they believe these judgments are generally correct. Other people do not judge a person's character quickly because they believe first impressions are often wrong. Tell about a time when your first impression of a person ended up being mistaken. Support your answer with specific examples.

Preparation time

00 : 00 : 00

Preparation time: 30 seconds
Response time: 60 seconds

Question 2

Section
Speaking

Question
2 of 6

Testing Tools
Volume Back Next Help

Do you agree or disagree with the following statement? People should read only those books that are about real events, real people, and established facts. Use specific reasons and details to support your opinion.

Preparation time

00 : 00 : 00

Preparation time: 30 seconds
Response time: 60 seconds

Question 3

Narrator: A university is advertising its Career Services Center. Read the following bulletin about the center. You will have 45 seconds to read the bulletin. Begin reading now.

Reading time: 45 seconds

Your Career Begins Here!

The University Career Services Center has a variety of services for students at all levels of career development. The center offers two virtual e-courses, Orientation 151 and Orientation 252, to assist students in planning their careers. The center's Jobs Location and Development Office houses an extensive collection of job and internship postings. This year, the center is offering three new services: career shadowing and career mentoring programs, as well as virtual e-fairs. We also offer weekly "career advice" via the Career LifeLine and host employment expos, job fairs, and summer job fairs throughout the campus. Browse through our web pages and resources to discover why your career begins here.

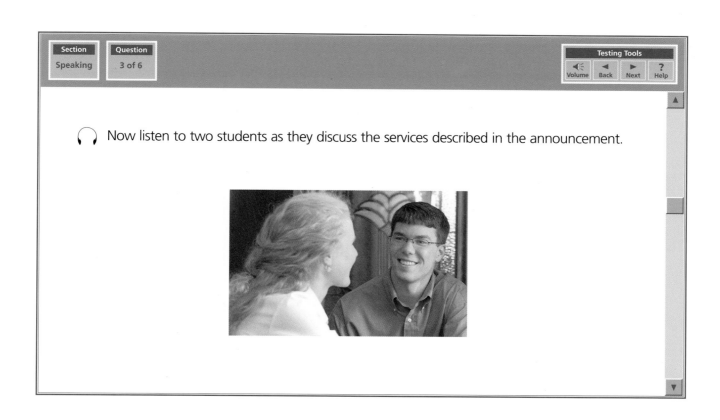

Now listen to two students as they discuss the services described in the announcement.

The woman expresses her opinion of the Career Services Center. State her opinion and explain the reasons she gives for holding that opinion.

Preparation time

00 : 00 : 00

Preparation time: 30 seconds
Response time: 60 seconds

Question 4

Narrator: Now read the following passage about the Earth's interior. You have 45 seconds to read the passage. Begin reading now.

Reading time: 45 seconds

The Layers of the Earth

The Earth is composed of four main layers: the inner core, the outer core, the mantle, and the crust. At the center of the Earth lies the core. In fact, the core is made up of two parts: the inner core and the outer core. These layers differ in that the outer core is molten, but the inner core is solid due to the extreme pressure at the center of the Earth. Above the core is the mantle, the layer in which most of the Earth's mass is found. The crust is much thinner than either the core or the mantle. The crust is rocky and brittle. Thus, it is susceptible to fracture, as happens during earthquakes.

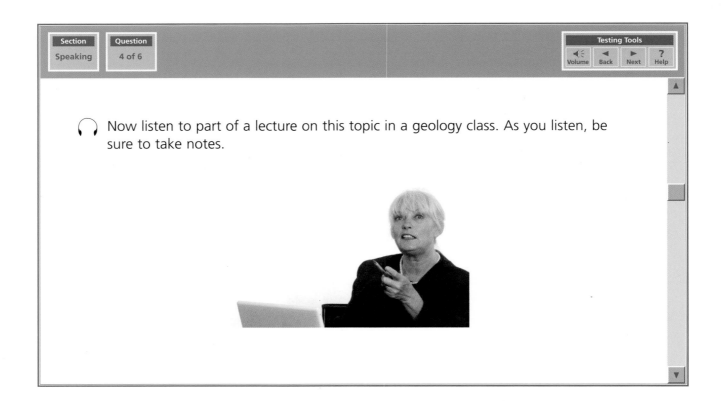

Now listen to part of a lecture on this topic in a geology class. As you listen, be sure to take notes.

The professor describes additional information not mentioned in the reading. Explain how the information in the lecture relates to the information in the reading.

Preparation time

00 : 00 : 00

Preparation time: 30 seconds
Response time: 60 seconds

Question 5

Section
Speaking

Question
5 of 6

Testing Tools
Volume Back Next Help

🎧 Now listen to a conversation between two students.

Section
Speaking

Question
5 of 6

Testing Tools
Volume Back Next Help

The students discuss two possible solutions to the man's problem. Describe the problem. Then state which of the two solutions you prefer and explain why.

Preparation time

00 : 00 : 00

Preparation time: 30 seconds
Response time: 60 seconds

Question 6

Section
Speaking

Question
6 of 6

Testing Tools
Volume Back Next Help

🎧 Now listen to part of a lecture in a health class.

Using points and examples from the lecture, explain the basic theory behind Chinese medicine.

Preparation time

00 : 00 : 00

Preparation time: 30 seconds
Response time: 60 seconds

Transcripts

Chapter 1

Skill A

Q1 — practice 1

Sample response:
Lance Armstrong is my role model for several reasons. First, he is a cyclist who has won the Tour de France seven times in a row. That, however, is not the only reason I respect this man. He also battled cancer. When I heard his story, it changed my life. Lance Armstrong inspired me to never give up on my dream of going to the Olympics, even though it may seem impossible. His qualities of endurance and perseverance compelled me to become a better athlete and a stronger person.

Q1 — practice 2

Sample response:
One gadget that has helped me with schoolwork is my "reading pen." To begin, I have dyslexia, a learning disability that makes reading very difficult. The reading pen was of great assistance to me. It scans words on a page and reads them out loud to me. I used it every day to help me with my reading assignments. Without it, I would have spent hours reading my assignments and wouldn't have had time to study properly. Because of my reading pen, I was able to excel in school.

Q1 — practice 3

Sample response:
When I was a child, I used to play soccer and baseball. I feel that practicing these sports helped me greatly. The chief benefit was that competing in these sports made my body healthy, instilling me with endurance and strength. Playing baseball developed my upper body strength for hitting and throwing. Soccer, on the other hand, provided me with lower body strength for kicking and stamina and endurance for playing full 90-minute games. Developing a strong, healthy body when I was young has been crucial in maintaining my health later in life.

Q2 — practice 1

Sample response 1:
In my opinion, high school students should be required to follow a certain curriculum. This ensures students are exposed to a wide variety of subjects. If, for example, I had been permitted to select whatever courses I wanted, I would only have taken courses that I found diverting. In the long run, this would have limited my ability to pursue a medical career, which is what I'm doing now. Obviously, if I had been left to my own devices about choosing my courses, I would not be where I am today.

Sample response 2:
In my opinion, educators should let high school students decide which courses they want to study. This ensures that all students are in charge of their own destinies, and they should be permitted to determine their own academic paths. If, for example, a student prefers art to science, why should she waste her time studying science? In the long run, her efforts would be better spent on developing skills in a field that interests her. Obviously, if she has to direct part of her energy toward a course she doesn't like, she will have less time and energy to put toward her real interests.

Q2 — practice 2

Sample response 1:
Some celebrities become rich and famous and then return very little to society, while others attempt to use their influence to raise public awareness of a special cause, such as environmentalism or human rights. In my opinion, we are all better off heeding the expert advice of professionals and officials. After all, how much can a pop star really know about solving problems in Africa? Some people say stars can do a lot if they get behind a particular cause, and there may be some truth to that. However, expecting an erudite opinion from a pop star about health issues in Nigeria is a different matter.

Sample response 2:
Some celebrities become rich and famous and then return very little to society, while others attempt to use their influence to raise public awareness of a special cause, such as environmentalism or human rights. In my opinion, the least the public can do is carefully consider these views. After all, a person living at the top of society probably has a much better view of it and can see problems that normal people cannot. Some cynics contend that people should ignore well-known artists when they express their thoughts on global issues. However, I attribute these views to jealousy.

Q2 — practice 3

Sample response 1:
Some children begin helping out with household chores as soon as they are old enough, while others may never lift a finger. I personally feel that children should pitch in around the house as soon as possible. This teaches them the value of work and gives them a feeling of accomplishment and responsibility. Children who never have to assist around the house often become spoiled and grow up expecting others to do work for them. Parents may think they are helping their kids by doing their work for them, but in the long run, this is not the case.

Sample response 2:
Some children begin helping out with household chores as soon as they are old enough, while others may never lift a finger. I personally feel that childhood is a special time for learning and playing. This helps kids develop imagination, creativity, and social skills through interacting with friends. Children who have little time to enjoy childhood because they are doing work or chores are not given the opportunity to be young. Parents may think that they are teaching their kids responsibility, but in the long run, this lesson costs children more than it's worth.

Skill B

Q3 — practice 1

W: I heard they're going to start building that new Science Center soon.
M: That's right. They're starting on March 8th.
W: I don't know why they don't hold off until summer.
M: I think they want to have it finished before September when the new school year starts.
W: I know, but I teach a class in Clemens Hall like you. The cacophony from the construction is going to be really distracting.
M: Oh, didn't you see the announcement? They're going to relocate all of our classes.

W: Oh really? Well that allays my fears a bit. Maybe it's a wise decision after all. Where are we being moved to?

M: I don't know yet. We're supposed to get a memo once they figure it all out.

W: Well, I hope it's soon. It will take time to move all of our stuff.

Sample response:

The woman thinks that the university ought to wait until summer before they start building the new Science Center. Her concern is that the classes in nearby buildings, specifically, her class at Clemens Hall, will be distracted by the noise from the construction. However, when she talks to the man, he tells her that the university is planning on relocating the classes in Clemens Hall to other buildings on campus. When she learns this, she is relieved, and changes her mind about waiting until summer to commence construction on the new building.

Q3 — practice 2

M: Did you hear about this new anti-spam filter they're going to implement?

W: Yeah, I think it's tremendous. I abhor receiving spam. It wastes too much of my time.

M: My worry would be that it would block important mail, though. I mean, surely it will make mistakes from time to time.

W: Yes, of course, that's what your bulk folder is for.

M: Bulk folder?

W: Yes, according to the announcement, the anti-spam filter is only going to block mail that is obviously spam. If there's any incertitude, they will send it to your bulk folder.

M: Oh, so there's no chance that an email from a friend or from a potential employer will be misidentified as spam?

W: No, and it would be rare that something like that would be sent to your bulk folder.

M: OK. Well, if there's no risk involved, I think it's great, too.

Sample response:

The man and the woman are discussing a new anti-spam filter that will be installed at their university. The woman, who hates receiving spam, thinks it's a wonderful idea. The man, however, is concerned that the filter will make mistakes and accidentally block important mail. The woman assures him, though, that the filter has a safety feature. It only blocks mail that is obviously spam. If an incoming email looks suspicious, it is sent to the person's bulk folder. In the end, the man agrees that this system is probably safe and agrees with the woman that it is a good idea.

Q3 — practice 3

M: Hey June! Do you remember what the extra credit assignment was for our Web Design course?

W: Oh, yeah. Dr. Penrose said we could write a review of that guest speaker's presentation for 15 extra credit points.

M: Fifteen? Nice! Who's the speaker?

W: Oh, you know, James Brentworth, the high school whiz kid from San Diego who made a million dollars from his website.

M: Oh wow! THAT guy is gonna speak at our school? When?

W: There are announcements about it posted all over campus. It's gonna be Thursday night from seven to eight. I heard it's over in Selwidge Hall, next to the theater.

M: This should be a great opportunity. He probably has lots of useful counsel for future web designers. Plus, it's a freebie, right?

W: Yeah, and there's a question period afterwards, too.

M: Excellent! I'm going to prepare a few questions beforehand.

Sample response:

First, the man asks the woman for information on an extra credit assignment for a Web Design class they are both in. The woman then refers him to an announcement about a guest speaker, reminding him that they can earn credit for attending the talk. The man is excited about the opportunity for two reasons. First, he thinks the guest speaker will provide useful advice for aspiring web designers. In addition, he is pleased that there's no charge for admission to the speech. Therefore, he will prepare some questions to ask the speaker and attend the speech to receive extra credit.

Q4 — practice 1

W: You've all read about the Nash Equilibrium. Let's look at a real world situation to which a Nash Equilibrium might apply. Some seemingly insignificant choices in life become significant if people don't agree. For example, it doesn't matter if people drive on the left side of the road or on the right side, provided everyone agrees on one. Because of the risk of collision, it is in everyone's interest to adopt the same policy. Even during rush hour traffic, when drivers all want to get home as quickly as possible, and the left lane of oncoming traffic is empty, people will stay in the slow-moving right-hand lanes. In essence, these commuters are in competition with one another to get home as quickly as possible, yet each driver independently chooses the right side of the road because of the risk of failure or delay driving on the left side would pose.

Sample response:

The reading passage describes the Nash Equilibrium, a situation in competitions in which it is not in any competitor's interest to change strategy. The professor expounds on this idea by illustrating a real-life example of the Nash Equilibrium. This example refers to drivers in rush hour traffic. If each driver is considered a competitor, and driving on one side of the road as the strategy, then it fits the Nash Equilibrium. That is to say, it is not in a driver's interest to change strategy, given that a collision could hinder the success of that driver, and coincidentally, the other drivers, too.

Q4 — practice 2

M: The common view that the Black Plague was a strain of bubonic plague spread by fleas living on rats has come under renewed scrutiny in recent years. Several factors have led researchers to propose other microorganisms as the culprits for this pandemic. The first crucial piece of evidence comes from Iceland, where rats were not introduced until the 1800s. Despite this, Iceland was severely affected by the Black Plague long before 1800, but not by subsequent plagues known to have been spread by rats. Furthermore, the incubation period of the Black Plague (up to 30 days) and the rate at which it spread both point away from the bacterium *Yersinia pestis* as a logical cause. Some researchers have proposed pulmonary anthrax or the Ebola virus as more likely agents. Testing for these theories is still in its infancy, but forensic inspection of a 14th-century mass grave has revealed no traces of *Yersinia pestis*.

Sample response:

In the lecture, the professor discusses new theories about the cause of the Black Plague, a disease that killed two-thirds of Europeans in the 14th century. The traditional theory that it was bubonic plague spread to people by fleas carried on rats does not match up with some new evidence. First, Iceland was severely affected despite the fact it had no rats. Second, the incubation period and spreading of the disease differed from those typical of bubonic plagues. For these reasons, some researchers are now proposing other diseases as the cause, such as pulmonary anthrax or the Ebola virus.

Q4 — practice 3

W: I trust that you've all read in your textbooks that the Great Zimbabwe civilization was founded around the year 450 by ancestors of modern-day Shona speakers. This, however, has not always been the accepted interpretation of the archaeological evidence. After the British "discovery" of the ruins, British Imperialist officials became concerned. You see, the idea of a "black" civilization undermined the justification behind British Imperialism, namely, that whites were superior and that it was their duty to civilize other, "savage" peoples. Government officials commissioned a number of British archaeologists, including Bent and Hall, to investigate the site. Unfortunately, these men destroyed and plundered much of the ruins and officially concluded that the civilization had been built by foreigners from the north. Fortunately, however, archaeologist Randall-MacIver investigated the site in 1905, and her findings contradicted the earlier theories. The British Empire responded by banning archaeologists from the site for nearly 25 years! The racist myth about the ruins was not fully dispelled until Zimbabwe's independence in 1980.

Sample response:
The lecture discusses the rewriting of the history of the Great Zimbabwe civilization during the British Colonial period. The reading details the conclusions based on archaeological evidence. This evidence points to native Shona-speaking Africans as the founders of the civilization that boasted cities, royalty, and a monumental wall. British officials, on the other hand, put forth an official view that the civilization must have been built by foreigners from the north. Their hired archaeologists destroyed evidence and supported racist theories to justify imperialist ventures. Finally, after Zimbabwe gained its independence from Britain in 1980, the myth was dispelled and the truth became accepted.

Skill C

Q5 — practice 1

M: Hey, Jill. You look a bit frazzled.
W: Yeah, well, I loaned my library card to a friend, and she's taken off for the holidays. Now, I have a monumental report due, and I need to borrow some books.
M: Gee, that's a tough one, but I guess there are a couple of things you can do.
W: Well, I thought I could just use the public library. That'd be quick, but they may not have all the books I need.
M: Yeah, that's one option. You could also try to find someone who'd let you use their library card.
W: Huh, I hadn't thought of that. Maybe I could ask around the dorms. There must be someone still around.
M: It might be worth a shot. I'd let you use mine, but I already have too many books checked out for research on my final presentation.
W: That's OK. At least I have a couple of ideas now.
M: Yeah, well, good luck with it. I'll see you around.

Sample response 1:
The woman's problem is that she does not have her university library card, but she needs to check out some books. The man and the woman discuss two options. The first option is that she just use the public library. The second option is that she try to find someone whose card she can borrow. I think the first option is better. She can go to the public library immediately without wasting any time looking for help. Also, there is no guarantee she would find anyone willing to be imposed upon, so the second option may be a waste of time.

Sample response 2:
The woman's problem is that she does not have her university library card, but she needs to check out some books. The man and the woman discuss two options. The first option is that she just use the public library. The second option is that she try to find someone whose card she can borrow. I think the second option is better. Chances are very good that she will find a friend more than happy to help her. Furthermore, the public library may not have the resources she needs, so it may be a waste of time to go there.

Q5 — practice 2

M: How's it going?
W: Not so good. My roommate is driving me crazy. She never cleans up after herself, and she always eats my food.
M: That's no good. You should talk to her about it!
W: The thing is, she's really sensitive, and I don't want to lose her as a friend.
M: You think complaining would put your friendship in jeopardy?
W: She can be really defensive. I wouldn't be surprised if she moved out and never spoke to me again.
M: Well, that sounds really manipulative to me. If you talk to her about it, I think you'll both be happier. Plus, you won't spend all your money feeding her.
W: But if she moves out, I'll have no help with the rent.
M: True. Well, if you can tough it out, graduation isn't that far off.
W: That's what I'm thinking. Then, I won't lose her friendship, and I won't have to spend the next two months bickering with her.

Sample response 1:
The woman is unhappy living with a friend who eats the woman's food and refuses to clean. The man admits the woman could just stick with the situation for a short time longer, but he recommends that she talk to her roommate about the problem. In my opinion, the woman should follow the man's recommendation. For one thing, it is not fair for her to have to do all the cleaning and pay for the food her roommate consumes. Also, if the woman convinces her roommate to start helping out, they will both be happier because there won't be any resentment between them.

Sample response 2:
The woman is unhappy living with a friend who eats the woman's food and refuses to clean. The man admits the woman could just stick with the situation for a short time longer, but he recommends that she talk to her roommate about the problem. In my opinion, the woman should follow her instincts and continue to live with her friend without complaint. For one thing, petty concerns are not worth losing a friend over. Also, if the roommate were to get upset and move out, the woman would be stuck paying all of the rent herself.

Q5 — practice 3

M: You took biology last year, right? Did you have to dissect a pig?

W: Yeah, it was gross.

M: I don't care if it's gross, I think it's wrong. I don't want to take part in it.

W: Why don't you explain your position to your teacher? Maybe he would give you an alternative project to do.

M: Yeah, but I'm scared he would hold it against me. You know, some teachers don't like troublemakers.

W: Well, I guess there's a chance that might happen. I guess you have to decide what is more important to you: your grades or your values. You can suck it up and do the dissection to ensure that you get a good grade, or you can stand up for what you believe in.

M: But you know that old saying about knowing when to stand and fight and knowing when to run.

W: You know what? There is power in numbers. If you can get your classmates to join your cause, you might actually bring about change. There's no reason why they can't do virtual dissections in biology class.

M: Hey, you know, you're right.

Sample response 1:
The man's biology class is going to dissect a pig, and he does not want to take part because he believes that dissecting pigs is unethical. The woman suggests that he refuse to take part in the dissection and ask his teacher for an alternative project to do. The man expresses concern, though, that the teacher might be annoyed with him and lower his grade because of it. I believe the man should stick to his convictions and not take part in activities that contravene his beliefs. He will feel better about himself, and protesting might result in change.

Sample response 2:
The man's biology class is going to dissect a pig, and he does not want to take part because he believes that dissecting pigs is unethical. The woman suggests that he refuse to take part in the dissection and ask his teacher for an alternative project. The man expresses concern, though, that the teacher might be annoyed with him and lower his grade because of it. I believe the man should dissect the pig and not risk getting a poor grade. He will only have to dissect the pig once, but a poor grade will cause him problems in the future.

Q6 — practice 1

M: So, today we're going to talk about falconry. This is a hunting method where the hunter, known as the falconer, trains a falcon to find and catch prey for him. Yes?

W: See, to me that's not hunting. It's like the fox hunt... you get another animal to do the hunting for you. Where's the skill in that?

M: OK, well, for one thing, taming a wild bird is no easy task. Indeed, part of that training lies in teaching the bird not to kill the prey. You see, in Arabia, where falconry still takes place, the prey must be killed according to Islamic customs and rituals. Therefore, it's not as if the falconer is passive during the hunt sequence. Now, let's talk about falconry in a historic context. While today it is a sport, when falconry began, it was an important means of survival. For example, nomadic people who traveled the desert needed to eat. The kinds of foods that they could procure for themselves were lacking in variety. Consequently, they enlisted one of the local hunters, the falcon, to help them add the dietary variety needed for subsistence. Some historians assert that falconry may have been the earliest hunting method developed by man. It was in use as far back as 2000 B.C. in China.

Sample response:
Falconry was originally employed as a tool to help people hunt food. Nomadic people in the desert tamed falcons in order to help them hunt for a larger variety of foods than they could acquire by themselves. Today, in contrast, people aren't as desperate to meet subsistence requirements. Nonetheless, falconry is still practiced as a sport. The falconer is highly skilled and must not only tame the falcon, but also teach it to hunt without killing the prey.

Q6 — practice 2

W: Any migraine sufferers here today?

M: I am.

W: Do you have auras?

M: Yes, I see flashing lights.

W: For those of you who don't know, "aura" refers to symptoms that precede an actual migraine. Sam says he sees flashing lights before his migraines set in. That's a common type of aura. So, Sam, what happens next?

M: Within about an hour, I'll have an incredible headache, and I'll start vomiting.

W: Does noise bother you?

M: Not as much as light. I have to find a dark room to rest in because I can't stand light.

W: That's common as well. So, that's what a migraine is . . . an intense headache accompanied by other symptoms. Not everyone gets them, but those who do get them episodically. Which leads us to the question "What causes migraines?" Well, medical science is not really sure, but we think it has something to do with blood flow in the brain. Basically, for some reason, some people's blood vessels respond in a weird way to certain stimulants. Arteries that bring blood to the brain contract and limit the blood supply, which means that less oxygen is getting to the brain. This problem is compounded because arteries in the brain will expand to compensate, and that expansion causes pain. So, the trick to preventing migraines is figuring out what triggers the arteries to contract in the first place.

Sample response:
A migraine is a severe headache that may be preceded by an aura, a symptom that signals the sufferer to the onset of a migraine. The migraine itself involves a headache and other symptoms, such as vomiting or intolerance for light or noise. Doctors suspect a possible cause is that restricted blood flow to the brain causes oxygen levels in the brain to decrease. The brain then tries to compensate by expanding the arteries in the brain, which results in pain. Migraine sufferers should try to identify what triggers their migraine to prevent further attacks.

Q6 — practice 3

M: You all should be familiar with the standard view of evolution. That is, that species change gradually over time as a result of natural selection until a new species is eventually formed. Who can give me an example?

W: Size?

M: OK, good. A species, like horses for instance, may grow from being the size of cats to the size of a modern horse over tens of thousands of years. The change in each particular generation is imperceptible, perhaps less than a nanometer. However, the fossil record holds evidence of another trend as well. This is the trend for populations to remain relatively unchanged over long periods of time, and then for new species to develop quite suddenly. A new idea in evolutionary theory attempts to account for this. It is called

Punctuated Equilibrium. In Punctuated Equilibrium theory, a large population typically dilutes advantageous mutations. According to this theory, the evolution of new species typically occurs in peripheral subpopulations, in smaller areas in which individuals are competing in novel ecosystems. In these populations, advantageous mutations can quickly take over. After this change, the new species may or may not compete with and exterminate its predecessor. I want to make it clear that this theory is not in conflict with the gradualist view of evolution. In fact, it complements it.

Sample response:
The professor explains two theories of evolution: one related to gradual evolution and the other related to rapid evolution. One example presented is the evolution of horses from cat-sized mammals to their much larger modern stature. This example supports the theory of gradual evolution. However, evidence in the fossil record indicates that species often remain unchanged for long periods, and then new species arise quite suddenly. Punctuated Equilibrium is a new theory that explains this. It holds that large populations dilute new mutations. On the other hand, beneficial mutations spread quickly in peripheral subpopulations. The professor points out that the two theories complement rather than contradict each other.

Chapter 2

Skill A

Q1 — practice 1
Sample response:
Last year, I met a fellow language student on an Internet study forum when I was trying to practice for a Chinese class. As it turned out, he was a Chinese student trying to practice English. Later, we developed a symbiotic relationship by helping each other practice our respective languages. Every week, we chat for 30 minutes in English and 30 minutes in Chinese. By now, we have become good friends, and we have both learned a lot. Of course, among the things I've learned is the fact that Chinese culture is fascinating, and this experience has really broadened my view of the world.

Q1 — practice 2
Sample response:
One technological innovation I witnessed during my university days was the spread of the Internet. Before that, I spent hours in the library doing research. After the Internet came into widespread use, however, I didn't have to go to the library at all. I could do all of my research from a computer in my dorm room, which saved a lot of time. In fact, the Internet saved me a great deal of money, too! For example, I no longer had to make expensive, obligatory phone calls to my parents. Instead, I could send them updates via email for free.

Q1 — practice 3
Sample response:
My life was changed by an unexpected blizzard. One day when I left my house to go to the airport, the weather was cool but clear. As I was driving to the airport, though, it started snowing. Within minutes, there was a raging blizzard. I knew my flight to Jamaica was going to be canceled, so I was terribly disappointed. Then, I noticed a stranded motorist, so I pulled over to help. I offered the man a lift so he could call a tow truck. Three years later, I married that man. If it weren't for that blizzard, we wouldn't have met.

Q1 — practice 4
Sample response:
The Optimists' Club is an organization that has been very important in my life. They organize fun and enriching activities for kids in the city. For example, I had a great experience and forged lasting friendships while participating in their youth basketball league. In addition, they provide counselors who help troubled youths with problems. One time, I was on edge about my high school course work, and I did not have anyone to turn to for guidance. The Optimists' Club counselor provided me with some very useful advice I needed in order to select the appropriate classes to enroll in.

Q2 — practice 1
Sample response:
I believe that childhood is a critical period in a person's life. First, it is the time in which personality is developed. Second, a person's experiences in childhood affect the remainder of his or her life. For instance, a major trauma experienced at the age of six has a much more devastating effect than one experienced at age thirty. Indeed, negative or traumatic experiences in childhood can lead to psychological problems in adulthood, such as depression and antisocial behavior. Conversely, positive, nurturing experiences in childhood foster mental health and well-being in adulthood. Thus, it is crucial to have positive influences in childhood.

Q2 — practice 2
Sample response:
Most parents are capable of teaching their children to read, write, add, and subtract, as well as many of the other basic skills children are taught at school. However, there are some skills that cannot be taught sufficiently at home. The skills I am referring to are social skills. These, I believe, are the most important skills learned at school. That's why I am of the opinion that children should learn in a social environment. Unfortunately, the home cannot provide an adequate social milieu for children to learn to live with a diverse group of people. Public schools, on the other hand, can and do provide this setting.

Q2 — practice 3
Sample response:
I believe zoos serve a multitude of useful purposes. For one thing, zoos educate visitors. If there were no zoos, children would grow up never witnessing species not indigenous to their area. With zoos, in contrast, children can learn about all kinds of different animal species and observe them up close. That's more captivating and educational than looking at pictures or reading texts. For that matter, zoos provide an entertainment venue for people of all ages. Additionally, they provide a safe home for animals whose survival is threatened in the wild. Animals that are endangered can be kept safe and well fed, as well as be encouraged to breed.

Q2 — practice 4
Sample response:
In some countries, all citizens are required to vote, while in others, individuals are free to decide whether to vote or not. I prefer the system in which voting is optional. First, in this system, public interest is more

important because it affects voter turnout. Therefore, governments and candidates for office must work harder to sway the opinions of voters. Second, people should be free to protest an election by refraining from taking part. Indeed, the very idea of forcing constituents to vote runs counter to the principles upon which free society is based.

Skill B

Q3 — practice 1

W: Darn! I really wanted to apply for the Study Abroad Program, but I can't afford it.

M: The tuition cost is no different from what you'd pay here.

W: Yeah, but I'm here on scholarship, and it can't be used toward tuition abroad.

M: I thought the announcement said that it could.

W: Only if it's need-based. Mine's academic.

M: That's so arbitrary and unfair.

W: I know. Technically, my scholarship isn't need-based, but I do need it.

M: I could fathom them precluding a person with an athletic scholarship from going, but you earned that scholarship.

W: There's not much I can do about it. They have their rules.

M: It doesn't make any sense, though. What difference does it make to them if your scholarship is based on academic merit or need? Why should a C student with poor parents have an advantage? I'm all for helping people out with university costs, but it's not fair that they can use their grant money and you can't.

W: Funny thing is, I qualified for a need-based scholarship, but I got more money with the academic one.

M: Well, there you go. There's no reason why you should be excluded from this program. You're an A student with financial needs.

Sample response:
The man's opinion is that the school's policy of only allowing students with need-based scholarships to use that money toward the Study Abroad Program is unfair. To begin, he contends that the woman earned her scholarship through academic merit rather than athletic skill or financial need. Secondly, the woman did qualify for a need-based scholarship but opted for the academic one, showing that she has the same financial need as students with need-based scholarships. For these two reasons, he feels the woman should be allowed to use her grant money to pay for tuition abroad.

Q3 — practice 2

M: I guess we'd better sign up for that lottery.

W: I can't believe this. It just doesn't seem fair. Why should people studying sociology get preferential treatment?

M: Who knows? I suppose they bring more prestige to the school. Maybe they pull in more research grant dollars. These things are usually all about the money.

W: It should be based on need. I'm just barely getting by on my grant as it is. Now, some kids whose parents have two houses are gonna get a dorm room and I'm not?

M: You might still get a room. Anyway, they said they'd give us a refund for living costs.

W: They said a partial tuition refund. I doubt it'll cover the cost of renting a place in this city, especially near the campus. Then, I'll have transportation costs on top of everything else, and I won't be able to stay at the library too late because I'll have to catch the last bus home.

M: Huh. I never thought about all that.

W: I should go give them a piece of my mind!

M: Yeah, but what can they do about it?

W: They should've done the renovations in the summer. Either that or made some other arrangements for their students.

Sample response:
The woman is angry about the announced plan for a housing lottery for graduate students. First, she thinks it is unfair because students of certain majors are being given priority. Instead, she believes the housing should be assigned based on need. Second, she is upset because living off campus will be expensive and inconvenient. For example, she will pay more in rent and transportation and will not be able to study late on campus. In the end, she complains that they should have done the renovations during the summer or otherwise accommodated the needs of all students.

Q4 — practice 1

W: The giant squid has proven a particularly elusive animal. In fact, marine biologists have tried in vain to conduct detailed studies of giant squid behavior for decades. The majority of what science knows about this species has been gleaned from the examination of dead squid carcasses washed up on shore.
Giant squid, as the name implies, are huge creatures. The largest specimen ever discovered measured fifteen meters in length. However, most giant squid are smaller, growing to approximately ten meters. They boast two large tentacles in addition to their eight arms. These tentacles have suckers, like that of an octopus, with sharp, claw-like components. They do not possess the stingers or net-like mechanisms for trapping prey commonly found on passive feeders.
Despite this, their enormous size has led some scientists to propose that giant squid are indeed passive feeders. Some theorists contend that, because of the energy requirements for such a large creature to move quickly enough to capture prey, it must, by necessity, be a passive feeder. Other theorists, needless to say, are not sympathetic to this view. Given the evidence presented by the physical morphology of the animal in conjunction with the feeding paradigm of its smaller cousins, it seems feasible that the giant squid may be an active feeder.

Sample response:
The reading passage describes the morphological differences between marine animals that are active feeders and passive feeders. The lecturer examines the morphology of the giant squid and different theories about its feeding habits. First, the giant squid is a very large creature. Second, it has two tentacles that include sharp, claw-like components. Some scientists have postulated that the enormous size of the giant squid suggests it must be a passive feeder. Other scientists, in contrast, point to its tentacles and the model of smaller squid species as evidence suggesting that the giant squid is an active feeder.

Q4 — practice 2

M: In the early 20th century, there was uproar in the musical world. European concert-goers were plugging their ears, walking out on performances, and muttering, "My Lord, what is that horrible, unstructured sound?"
That unstructured sound was the new, emerging style of European composition. It came to be known as atonal music. Basically, it was the beginning of a rebellion against the way music had always been. All the rules were going out the window, music fans were lambasting the composers, and the composers were replying

that the fans were uncouth or needed more time and education to understand the new musical form.

So, how was their music so different? Well, let's think about the traditional way of arranging music. You use a scale, right? And you build the composition, or song, around that scale. The traditional scales were the major and minor scales. Well, these new composers started using the chromatic scale to structure their music. The chromatic scale means simply all the notes you can play on a piano, without any notes left out. The traditional scales had eight notes in total, and now they were using all 12 notes in the same composition!

Sample response:

The professor begins by describing the negative response many early-20th-century audiences had to the advent of atonal musical forms. Listeners found the new style too unstructured in comparison to the traditional forms they were used to. As the reading passage describes, traditional European music was based on principles of melody. This music utilized the major and minor scales to produce the desired emotions. As the professor points out, atonal compositions utilized the chromatic scale rather than the major or minor scales. The chromatic scale includes 12 notes, all the notes a person can play on the piano.

Skill C

Q5 — practice 1

M: Hi, is this the Student Administrative Services Center?

W: Yes, it is. What can I help you with?

M: Well, there seems to be some kind of glitch with my ID card. The scanner at the gym wouldn't read it, and they told me to come here to find out why.

W: Have you got your student ID on you?

M: Yeah, it's right here.

W: OK, let's get your record up on the computer...Bill Hailey, here it is. It seems you haven't paid your tuition yet.

M: Yeah, my loan hasn't come through yet.

W: Unfortunately, until you've paid in full, your status is not active.

M: Oh. Can I just pay the fee?

W: Sorry, you must have active status to use the facilities. If you know someone who does have access, you can go as his or her guest for five dollars.

M: Five dollars? OK, well, I guess I'll have to do that. I'm in training and I need to use the gym.

W: Keep in mind that your host has to be in the facility with you.

M: Gee, that's a pain in the neck.

W: You said you were in training; are you on a varsity team here?

M: Yeah, the basketball team.

W: Why don't you talk to your coach? Maybe you could get a temporary ID until your loan comes through.

M: Hmmm...my coach is away right now. Well, thanks for all you're help, anyway.

Sample response:

The man's problem is that he cannot access the gym to work out because his student loans have not come through to pay his tuition. The woman suggests two solutions to his problem. First, he could find a student with access to accompany him to the gym. Second, he could talk to his coach and try to get a temporary ID. In my opinion,

the first choice is preferable. To begin, his coach is away, so the man would have to wait. In addition, having a friend to work out with could help him maintain his exercise regime.

Q5 — practice 2

W: Richard. Long time no see.

M: Yeah, I've had some personal problems. I'm here to drop the class.

W: You know you've missed the deadline to drop a class without penalty?

M: I know, but I really don't see how I could catch up this late in the game.

W: Let me have a look... no term paper and a D on the midterm.

M: Like I said, I've had some personal problems.

W: Still, there's no advantage to dropping the class now. On the other hand, if you put your nose to the grindstone from here on out, you might pull off a C.

M: Hmm. Would you give me an extension on the paper?

W: Sorry. You'll be docked two points per day like everyone else.

M: Yeah, well, I think I'd rather just drop it.

W: Suit yourself, but dropping a course now is no different from failing it. Why don't you just give it a shot?

M: Well, I'll think about it. The thing is, if I drop this class, I can concentrate on the classes I'm taking for my major.

W: OK, but don't think too long. If you want to pass the class, you should turn in that paper ASAP.

Sample response:

The man's problem is that he wants to drop the professor's class because he is too far behind to earn a high grade. In addition, the deadline for dropping classes without penalty has passed. The professor tries to convince him to remain in the class and work hard to increase his grade. In my opinion, he would be better off dropping the class. Even though he will be penalized for dropping the class the same as if he had failed it, he will benefit by being able to concentrate his efforts on the courses of his major.

Q6 — practice 1

W: The most influential development in popular music history was undoubtedly the advent of jazz and its later incarnation, blues. Jazz and blues music originated in New Orleans, Louisiana, when African-American musicians broke free from the musical norms of that period. Jazz and blues artists combined faster, more powerful African rhythms with European melodies. They are also credited with the development of the "blues" scale, which uses the major scale with an extra note, the "blue" note. This music, however, was not widely accepted by mainstream America at the time. The wild, unstructured style of jazz was too much for them, just as later, the intoxicating beat of rock 'n' roll was met with disapproval. However, when white musicians such as Elvis Presley began incorporating these new styles into their music, it became wildly popular with the younger generations. As these generations grew up, rock 'n' roll eventually became universally accepted.

Subsequent developments in pop music were generally met with the same disapproval experienced by jazz, blues, and rock 'n' roll in their infancies. One example of this is hip-hop, which appeared on the scene in the early 1980s. It is based on poetic verses spoken over heavy backbeats, which include samples from other songs and repeated noises not produced by traditional instruments, such as police sirens and record scratches.

Pop music today is a fusion of a myriad of styles that did not exist 100 years ago. Many of the most popular bands on the charts today are born from influences of rock, hip-hop, reggae, ska, and techno, all of which met with resistance in their infancies.

Sample response:
According to the lecture, the advent of jazz music had a significant influence on the trajectory of popular music over the past 100 years. To begin, it was developed by African Americans combining African rhythms with European melodies. In addition, jazz influenced the development of blues, which added an extra note to the major scale, thus creating the blues scale. At first, these musical forms were met with resistance. Later, however, they became widely accepted after being incorporated into rock 'n' roll music by white musicians such as Elvis Presley. Furthermore, they have influenced the form of more recent popular music styles, such as hip-hop.

Q6 — practice 2

M: What images are conjured in people's minds when the word "family" is mentioned? It's difficult to pinpoint these days, isn't it? We can regurgitate the ideal family of our parents' generation, though, right? You know: Mom, Dad, and 2.5 children. Dad works nine to five. Mom takes Dad's family name, serves as his companion, and stays at home to cook, clean, and raise the children. They remain married until one of them dies. Sex only occurs inside the confines of marriage. Parents have the ultimate say in the lives of their children. Does that work for you?

In the past, families who did not conform to this paradigm were marginalized. They were considered "troubled," "pathological," or "dysfunctional." In the 1960s, about 70 percent of all families conformed to the ideal, leaving 30 percent in the "problematic" range.

Today, only 11-15 percent of families adhere to the above conditions for the ideal family. It appears this conception of family is disappearing. Some alarmists contend that this is a fundamental societal problem, a breakdown in values that will produce immeasurable negative effects. Is this true?

Well, let's look at it from another angle. There are myriad cultures around the world that have never held this ideal of the family. Even in the American past, the family has been defined differently depending on the time period. So, it seems that what was briefly the ideal family unit was just another phase.

We can cite a few aspects of family that apply universally. Family is the intersection between social reproduction, that is, making a society, and biological reproduction, that is, making new people. The concept of family is what provides a society with its notions of "normal" and "natural."

Sample response:
In this lecture, the professor examines the idea of family. The traditional ideal of the family includes a working father, a domestic mother, and two or three children all living together in one home. Furthermore, families that differed from this ideal were marginalized and considered flawed or unhealthy in the past. These days, however, only a minority of families conform to this ideal. In point of fact, the professor relates that the ideal defined a generation or two ago is only one step on an ever-evolving sequence of ideals. Finally, the professor states that in all societies, the family helps define what is normal and natural.

Chapter 3

Focus A

Step 1 — Sentence stress on content words
1. Before that, I spent hours in the library doing research.
2. My life was changed by an unexpected blizzard.
3. In addition, they provide counselors who help troubled youths with problems.
4. I believe that childhood is an integral period in a person's life.
5. Public schools, on the other hand, can and do provide this setting.
6. That's more captivating and educational than looking at pictures or reading texts.
7. I prefer the system in which voting is optional.
8. Instead, she believes the housing should be assigned based on need.

Paragraph:
I believe zoos serve a multitude of useful purposes. For one thing, zoos educate visitors. If there were no zoos, children would grow up never witnessing species not indigenous to their area. With zoos, in contrast, children can learn about all kinds of different animal species and observe them up close. That's more captivating and educational than looking at pictures or reading texts. For that matter, zoos provide an entertainment venue for people of all ages. Additionally, they provide a safe home for animals whose survival is threatened in the wild. Animals that are endangered can be protected, well-fed, and encouraged to breed.

Step 2 — Sentence stress on function words
1. Technically, my scholarship isn't need-based, but I do need it.
2. If you put your nose to the grindstone from here on out, you might pull off a C.
3. After the Internet came along, I could do all of my research from a computer in my dorm room.
4. First, it is the time in which personality is developed.
5. However, there are some skills that cannot be taught sufficiently at home.
6. Public schools, on the other hand, can and do provide this setting.
7. In my opinion, the second choice is preferable.
8. Although no specimens have been found, there is a lot of evidence for scientists to examine.

1. That isn't his dog, it's her dog.
2. Most students didn't pass the exam, but John did.
3. She likes jazz music, and he likes blues music. I like jazz and blues music.
4. Kim hasn't paid her tuition fees, but Rick has.
5. The major scale doesn't have 12 notes, but the chromatic scale does.
6. Off-campus housing isn't just expensive; it's expensive and inconvenient.
7. He didn't get the need-based scholarship. She did.
8. You can take English 201 or English 205. You can't take both.

Focus B

Step 1 — Changing pitch for emphasis

1. Children should attend school.
2. This experience helped tremendously with my studies.
3. Subsequent developments in pop music were generally met with the same disapproval.
4. Do you play on the varsity basketball team?

1. I don't abhor jazz music. I don't really enjoy it that much, though.
2. Her behavior is antisocial. He is actually a nice guy.
3. The squid doesn't have eight appendages. It has ten.
4. Jellyfish drift with ocean currents. Squid use their arms to swim.
5. There is a glitch with her computer. Her phone is working fine.
6. The campus renovations will begin in September. The campus celebrations begin in October.

Step 2 — Commas and series with *and* or *or*

1. Many of the most popular bands on the charts today are born from influences of rock, hip-hop, reggae, ska, and techno.
2. They were considered troubled, pathological, or dysfunctional.
3. I doubt it'll cover the cost of renting a place in this city, especially near the campus.
4. Most giant squid are smaller, growing to approximately ten meters.
5. European concert-goers were plugging their ears, walking out on performances, and muttering to themselves.
6. The chromatic scale simply means all the notes you can play on a piano, without any notes left out.

Focus C

Step 1 — Timing

1. The traditional ideal of the family includes a working father, a domestic mother, and two or three children all living happily in one home.
2. As it turned out, he was a Chinese student trying to practice English.
3. After the Internet came into widespread use, however, I didn't have to go to the library at all.
4. Within minutes, there was a raging blizzard.
5. Some alarmists contend that this is a fundamental societal problem, a breakdown in values that will produce immeasurable negative effects.
6. These, I believe, are the most important skills learned at school.

1. The man's opinion is that the school's policy of only allowing students with need-based scholarships to use that money toward the Study Abroad Program is unfair.
2. To begin, he contends that the woman earned her scholarship through academic merit rather than athletic skill or financial need.
3. Secondly, the woman did qualify for a need-based scholarship but opted for the academic one, showing that she has the same financial need as students with need-based scholarships.
4. For these two reasons, he feels the woman should be allowed to use her grant money to pay for tuition abroad.

Step 2 — Pause and pitch

1. The reading passage describes the morphological differences between marine animals that are active feeders and passive feeders.
2. The lecturer examines the morphology of the giant squid and different theories about its feeding habits.
3. First, the giant squid is a very large creature.
4. Second, it has two tentacles that include sharp, claw-like components.
5. Some scientists have postulated that the enormous size of the giant squid suggests it must be a passive feeder.
6. Other scientists, in contrast, point to its tentacles and the model of smaller squid species as evidence suggesting the giant squid is an active feeder.

Practice Test

Question 3

M: Have you ever used any of the services offered by the Career Services Center?

W: I've never logged on to any of the e-fairs, but I have used the career mentoring program. It's great! I've been talking to this cool counselor at the Career Center, and he thinks I would be great in statistics or accounting.

M: Oh yeah? How does he know that?

W: He gave me a couple of tests to measure my interests and abilities. Then, he asked me lots of questions about the type of student I am, and what kind of lifestyle I want to have after I graduate. Then, he ran a computer cross-check that showed my skills and interests were most closely related to students who have majored in stats and accounting.

M: But what about finding a job when you graduate?

W: The Career Center also has a huge research database. The counselor told me there'll be lots of jobs in those two fields over the next 10 years.

M: It sounds good, but what if you declare one of those majors and then don't like it?

W: Well, the center can help me find an internship next summer. I can do volunteer work for a company in my major and see if I like it. If I don't, I can change my major. The counselor said the center will be glad to help. It's a great place. You should check it out!

Question 4

W: So, I think we've covered all there is to say about the core and the mantle. Those layers are quite familiar to students anyway. I want to take some time today to go into more detail about the Earth's crust. The description in the textbook is rather superficial. It basically describes the crust as a unified unit — I mean, you might get the impression that the crust is a homogenous layer, but it's not. The crust is actually better described as consisting of two parts: the continental crust and the oceanic crust. As you might guess from the names of these layers, the oceanic crust is the part under the oceans, and the continental crust is the part under the continents. Now, there are several interesting differences between these two parts of the crust, other than where they are located. One difference is the thickness. The continental crust is thicker than the oceanic crust. Also, the rocks found in the continental crust are older than the rocks found in the oceanic crust. Let's talk a bit about why this is the case.

Question 5

W: Hey, Ryan. What's new?

M: Hi, Jenny. Nothing much.

W: Everything OK? You seem kind of down.

M: I got this notice today. I'm on academic probation.

W: Probation?! Why? Your grades have been great!

M: Most of them are, but I failed geology.

W: Why?

M: Well, first I signed up for too many classes: 18 credit hours. Then, I got sick and fell behind in my economics class. That's my major. I had to write this big term paper. I also had to write another paper for my literature class, so I was concentrating on those. I just didn't have time to study geology.

W: Why didn't you drop it and take it again later?

M: I was going to, but like I said, I was sick for awhile, and I missed the deadline to drop classes. Man, I've never flunked a class in my life!

W: It'll be OK. Here's what you can do. You have two weeks to appeal to the college director. You can write him a letter and explain your circumstances. I'm sure when he hears what happened and looks at all your good grades, he'll take you off probation.

M: I could try, I guess, but I don't know . . . I don't really have a good excuse. It IS my fault. And I was only taking geology to fulfill a stupid science credit!

W: Your second choice is just to take the class again. You have one year. If you pass it, the new grade will replace the "F" on your transcripts.

M: Well, I could try that, but . . . um, the thing is, I don't know if I CAN pass it. It was hard!

W: Sure you can! You're smart, and I'll help you. Next semester, just don't take so many hours so you have more time to study. But Ryan, you've gotta do something — unless you want that "F" on your permanent record!

Question 6

M: Herbal treatments are important in traditional Eastern medicine. There are different medical traditions in different Eastern countries, but the most well-known in the West is probably Chinese medicine. It is common to find Chinese herbs at health-food stores in North America, and there are Chinese medical clinics in some cities. However, Chinese medicine has not been completely accepted by most American doctors. This is not because some herbal treatments are ineffective, but because of the basic theory behind Chinese medicine.

Traditional Chinese medical theory states that there is a power in the body called "chi." This power moves through the body along specific paths. If these paths are blocked, pain or disease can result. Chi can be hot or cold, active or passive, but there should not be too much of one or the other. The healthiest person has chi that is balanced and flows freely. Chi can be blocked or unbalanced in various ways. Many things can affect chi movement, such as food and body position as well as a person's mental and emotional state. Different herbs have different effects on chi. Ginseng, for example, can stimulate active chi, hence warming the body, while other herbs have a cooling effect. Combinations of various herbs can have complex effects.

Traditional Chinese medicine tries to affect chi first, before treating the symptoms of an illness. Western medicine treats the symptoms first. Therefore, traditional Chinese doctors claim that their way is useful for treating continuing problems and preventing disease, while Western medicine is better for problems that need urgent help. While many Western doctors agree that Chinese herbal treatments can be beneficial, few believe in the idea of chi. Since chi is invisible and its effects cannot be measured, there is no direct evidence for it. Until chi can be proved or disproved, there will be no agreement about it.

Answer Key

Chapter 1

Skill B

Q3 – practice 1

Step 1

Suggested keywords:
construction, Science Center, Clemens Hall, relocated, location

Sample restatement:
Construction on the new Science Center will begin soon. Classes in Clemens Hall will be relocated. Professors will find out where the new class locations will be, and they should advise their students of the change.

Step 2

Suggested keywords:
Science Center, distracting, announcement, relocate, memo

Sample restatement:
The woman complains that the noise from the construction of the new Science Center will be distracting. The man tells her about an announcement saying the classes in their building will be relocated. She asks him where the classes will be relocated to, and he tells her that they will be informed through a memo.

Step 3

— Original Opinion: The woman thinks the university should wait until summer to begin construction on the new Science Center.
— Reason: The noise will be distracting to classes in Clemens Hall.
— Why she changes her mind: The man informs her that the classes in Clemens Hall will be relocated.

Q3 – practice 2

Step 1

Suggested keywords:
anti-spam filter, spam, inbox, potential spam, bulk folder

Sample restatement:
The university will install an anti-spam filter that will reject spam and send potential spam to bulk folders instead of inboxes, where non-spam emails will be sent.

Step 2

Suggested keywords:
Anti-spam filter, block important mail, mistakes, bulk folder, obviously spam

Sample restatement:
The man is concerned about the new anti-spam filter. He is worried that it will occasionally make mistakes and block important mail. The woman assures him that only mail that is obviously spam will be blocked. If there is any doubt, it will be sent to the man's bulk folder.

Step 3

— Woman's opinion: The anti-spam filter is great.
— Reason: She hates spam because it wastes her time.
— Man's concern: Important email will be blocked. The man changes his mind.
— Reason: The anti-spam filter doesn't block mail unless it is obviously spam. Suspicious mail gets directed to a bulk folder.

Q3 – practice 3

Step 1

Suggested keywords:
guest speaker, Internet business, telecommerce, all students welcome, question-and-answer period

Sample restatement:
A successful young Internet businessperson will speak from 7 p.m. to 8 p.m. Thursday night in Selwidge Hall. All students are welcome. There will be a question-and-answer period after the speech.

Step 2

Suggested keywords:
15 extra credit points, review of speech, Thursday night from 7 to 8, Selwidge hall, open to all students

Sample restatement:
The man asks the woman about their extra credit assignment. She tells him he can write a review of James's speech for 15 extra credit points. The speech is Thursday night from seven to eight in Selwidge Hall. The man is enthusiastic about learning from the guest speaker.

Step 3

— The man wants information on: the extra credit assignment.
— The woman tells him he can: write a review of the speech.
— The man's opinion of the assignment is that: it is a great opportunity.
— Reason 1: The speaker will have lots of useful advice.
— Reason 2: It's completely free.
— The man will: prepare some questions in advance.

Q4 – practice 1

Step 1

Suggested keywords:
the Nash Equilibrium, maintain static strategies, rational conception, no collusion, benefits competing parties

Sample restatement:
The Nash Equilibrium describes a competitive situation in which all competitors benefit from not changing their strategies. Also, each competitor decides to maintain his or her strategy independently of the others.

Step 2

Suggested keywords:
real world, agree, side of the road, risk of collision, rush hour traffic

Sample restatement:
The professor illustrates the Nash Equilibrium by giving the example of which side of the road cars drive on. The drivers only want to get home as quickly as possible. They don't communicate with one another to decide which side to drive on; nevertheless, everyone drives on the same side.

Step 3

— Nash Equilibrium: Each competitor cannot improve his or her odds by changing strategies.
— Professor's example: People wanting to get home quickly all drive on one side of the road.
— How they relate: Each driver is a competitor. They will not improve their chances of arriving more quickly by driving on the other side of the road and risking collision.

Q4 – practice 2

Step 1

Suggested keywords:
Black Plague, two thirds, germ theory, parasitic fleas, public sanitation

Sample restatement:
The passage is about the Black Plague, a disease that killed two-thirds of the population of Europe in the 1300s. Germ theory later discovered that it was caused by a bacterium spread to humans by parasitic fleas. Public sanitation and new medicine helped destroy the disease.

Step 2

Suggested keywords:
Yersinia pestis, Iceland, incubation period, pulmonary anthrax, Ebola virus

Sample restatement:
The professor talks about new theories that the Black Plague was not caused by *Yersinia pestis*. Some researchers now think it was pulmonary anthrax or the Ebola virus. Iceland was affected by the first plague, even though there were no rats. The incubation period of the disease also makes some people think this disease was NOT spread by fleas on rats.

Step 3

— Common understanding: The Black Plague was a bubonic plague caused by the bacterium *Yersinia pestis*, which was spread by fleas on rats.
— New evidence 1: There were no rats in Iceland, yet it was affected by the Black Plague.
— New evidence 2: The Black Plague had a longer incubation period and spread more quickly than *Yersinia pestis*.
— New theories: 1: Pulmonary anthrax
                   2: Ebola virus

Q4 – practice 3

Step 1

Suggested keywords:
450 AD, Shona-speaking herders, Zimbabwe plateau, 1100-1450, great civilization

Sample restatement:
The passage discusses the Great Zimbabwe civilization. It was founded by Shona-speakers in 450 and reached its peak between 1100 and 1450, when it had a king and a monumental wall.

Step 2

Suggested keywords:

British Imperialism, foreigners from the north, archaeologists, destroyed and plundered, racist myth

Sample restatement:

British officials felt threatened by the idea of a civilization founded by Black Africans. It undermined their justifications for imperialism. They hired archaeologists who destroyed and plundered the ruins and then concluded that foreigners from the north had founded the civilization. After another archaeologist contradicted the official theory, the site was closed off. Eventually, people recognized the reality behind the racist myth.

Step 3

— First British investigation: archaeologists destroyed and plundered site
— Conclusion and result: foreigners from the north built the ruins
— Further investigation: archaeologists studied site again in 1905
— Conclusion and result: contradicted earlier findings, archaeologists banned from site
— Accepted idea today: ruins built by local Shona-speakers

Skill C

Q5 — practice 1

Step 1

Suggested answers:

Problem: The woman needs to get some books but does not have her university library card.
Solution 1:   Use the public library
Solution 2:   Try to borrow someone else's card

Step 2

Problem: She needs to get some books but does not have her university library card.
Best solution: Use the public library
Reason 1:   This is the quickest solution.
Reason 2:   The other solution will impose on someone.

Problem: She needs to get some books but does not have her university library card.
Best solution: Try to borrow someone else's card
Reason 1:   She will probably find someone to help her.
Reason 2:   The public library may not have adequate resources.

Q5 — practice 2

Step 1

Suggested answers:

Problem: The woman's roommate is untidy, and she eats her food.
Solution 1:   Talk to her about it.
Solution 2:   Say nothing and wait until the school year is over. Then, she won't have to live with her anymore.

Step 2

Problem: The woman's roommate is untidy, and she eats her food.
Best solution: Talk to the roommate and ask her to be more considerate.
Reason 1:   She will be happier if they resolve the problem.
Reason 2:   The woman will save money on food.

Problem: The woman's roommate is untidy, and she eats her food.
Best solution: Tolerate the roommate's behavior for two more months.
Reason 1:   Don't risk having her roommate move out.
Reason 2:   Keep her roommate as a friend.

Q5 — practice 3

Step 1

Problem: The man doesn't want to dissect a pig in biology class.
Solution 1:   Refuse to take part
Solution 2:   Dissect the pig

Step 2

Problem: The man doesn't want to dissect a pig in biology class.

Best Solution: Refuse to take part
Reason 1: Won't have to do something that he is morally opposed to
Reason 2: May bring about change in the school's practice

Problem: The man doesn't want to dissect a pig in biology class.
Best Solution: Dissect the pig
Reason 1: Stay on the teacher's good side
Reason 2: Won't risk getting a bad grade

Q6 — practice 1

Step 1
Falconry is: a way to hunt prey using a trained falcon
Falconers must:
    a) tame the falcon
    b) train the falcon not to kill the prey
Today falconry is: a sport
Historically, falconry was: a means of survival
Nomadic people in the desert: used falconry to add variety to their diets
Falconry dates back to: China in 2000 BC

Q6 — practice 2

Step 1
An aura is a symptom or set of symptoms that precede a migraine.
example: perception of flashing lights
Common characteristics of migraines:
    — bad headache
    — vomiting
    — bothered by noise
    — bothered by light
Process of migraine: Arteries bringing blood to the brain constrict → Less oxygen getting to the brain → Arteries in brain expand causing pain
Possible way to prevent migraines from occurring: Identify the triggers that cause the arteries to constrict and avoid them.

Q6 — practice 3

Step 1
Standard view of evolution: Species arise gradually over time due to natural selection.
Example: Horses used to be the size of small cats.
Counter-evidence: Source: Fossil record
Trend: Species remain unchanged for long periods of time.
    New species arise quickly.
New theory: Punctuated Equilibrium
    — Large populations typically dilute advantageous mutations.
    — Speciation occurs in peripheral subpopulations because they are smaller and are located in novel ecosystems.
    — After the change, the new species might compete with and exterminate the old species.
The new theory is not in conflict with the standard view.

Vocabulary Review

Review 1

1. (C)	2. (A)	3. (D)
4. (D)	5. (B)	6. (A)
7. (B)	8. (D)	9. (B)
10. (A)	11. (D)	12. (A)
13. (B)	14. (D)	15. (D)
16. gadget	17. dyslexia	18. diverting
19. perseverance	20. better off	21. (C)
22. (A)	23. (E)	24. (D)
25. (B)		

Review 2

1. (B)	2. (D)	3. (A)
4. (C)	5. (A)	6. (D)
7. (C)	8. (A)	9. (A)
10. (D)	11. (B)	12. (C)
13. (B)	14. (A)	15. (D)
16. asserts	17. imperceptible	18. dilute
19. peripheral	20. exterminate	21. pandemic
22. thrive	23. enlist	
24. complement	25. surrender	

Chapter 2

Skill A

Q1 – practice 1

Step 1

Transitions: by now, every week, last year, later, of course, as it turned out

Sentence Order: C, F, D, B, A, E

Step 2

Suggested answers:
1. They met on an Internet site for students studying languages.
2. They practice Chinese and English together.
3. It helped him appreciate Chinese culture and broadened his view of the world.

Step 3

Sample response:

Last year, I met a fellow language student on an Internet study forum when I was trying to practice for a Chinese class. As it turned out, he was a Chinese student trying to practice English. Later, we developed a symbiotic relationship by helping each other practice our respective languages. Every week, we chat for 30 minutes in English and 30 minutes in Chinese. By now, we have become good friends, and we have both learned a lot. Of course, among the things I've learned is the fact that Chinese culture is fascinating, and this experience has really broadened my view of the world.

Q1 – practice 2

Step 1

Transitions: after, however, for example, instead, before that, in fact

Sentence Order: C, F, A, D, G, B, E

Step 2

Suggested answers:
1. The speaker was studying at university when the Internet became commonly used.
2. The Internet allowed the speaker to do research from her dorm room.
3. The Internet allowed the speaker to communicate with her parents for free.

Step 3

Sample response:

One technological innovation I witnessed during my university days was the spread of the Internet. Before that, I spent hours in the library doing research. After the Internet came into widespread use, however, I didn't have to go to the library at all. I could do all of my research from a computer in my dorm room, which saved a lot of time. In fact, the Internet saved me a great deal of money, too! For example, I no longer had to make expensive, obligatory phone calls to my parents. Instead, I could send them updates via email for free.

Q1 – practice 3

Step 2

Sample response:

My life was changed by an unexpected blizzard. One day when I left my house to go to the airport, the weather was cool but clear. As I was driving to the airport, though, it started snowing. Within minutes, there was a raging blizzard. I knew my flight to Jamaica was going to be canceled, so I was terribly disappointed. Then, I noticed a stranded motorist, so I pulled over to help. I offered the man a lift so he could call a tow truck. Three years later, I married that man. If it weren't for that blizzard, we wouldn't have met.

Q1 – practice 4

Step 2

Sample response:

The Optimists' Club is an organization that has been very important in my life. They organize fun and enriching activities for kids in the city. For example, I had a great experience and forged lasting friendships while participating in their youth basketball league. In addition, they provide counselors who help troubled youths with problems. One time, I was on edge about my high school course work, and I did not have anyone to turn to for guidance. The Optimists' Club counselor provided me with some very useful advice I needed in order to select the appropriate classes to enroll in.

Q2 – practice 1

Step 1

Transitions: thus, conversely, for instance, first, second, indeed

Sentence Order: D, E, F, C, G, B, A

Step 2

Suggested answers:

1. The speaker's view is that childhood is the most important time of a person's life.
2. One reason is that childhood is when basic personality develops.
3. Another reason is that experiences in childhood affect the rest of a person's life.

Step 3

Sample response:

I believe that childhood is a critical period in a person's life. First, it is the time in which personality is developed. Second, a person's experiences in childhood affect the remainder of his or her life. For instance, a major trauma experienced at the age of six has a much more devastating effect than one experienced at age thirty. Indeed, negative or traumatic experiences in childhood can lead to psychological problems in adulthood, such as depression and antisocial behavior. Conversely, positive, nurturing experiences in childhood foster mental health and well-being in adulthood. Thus, it is crucial to have positive influences in childhood.

Q2 – practice 2

Step 1

Transitions: on the other hand, that's why, however, unfortunately

Sentence Order: D, F, B, A, E, G, C

Step 2

Suggested answers:

1. The speaker thinks parents can teach their kids academic skills, like reading, writing, and math.
2. The speaker thinks that parents cannot adequately teach their children social skills.
3. The speaker thinks children should be educated in a social setting, i.e. in schools.

Step 3

Sample response:

Most parents are capable of teaching their children to read, write, add, and subtract, as well as many of the other basic skills children are taught at school. However, there are some skills that cannot be taught sufficiently at home. The skills I am referring to are social skills. These, I believe, are the most important skills learned at school. That's why I am of the opinion that children should learn in a social environment. Unfortunately, the home cannot provide an adequate social milieu for children to learn to live with a diverse group of people. Public schools, on the other hand, can and do provide this setting.

Q2 – practice 3

Step 2

Sample response:

I believe zoos serve a multitude of useful purposes. For one thing, zoos educate visitors. If there were no zoos, children would grow up never witnessing species not indigenous to their area. With zoos, in contrast, children can learn about all kinds of different animal species and observe them up close. That's more captivating and educational than looking at pictures or reading texts. For that matter, zoos provide an entertainment venue for people of all ages. Additionally, they provide a safe home for animals whose survival is threatened in the wild. Animals that are endangered can be kept safe and well fed, as well as be encouraged to breed.

Q2 – practice 4

Step 2

Sample response:

In some countries, all citizens are required to vote, while in others, individuals are free to decide whether to vote or not. I prefer the system in which voting is optional. First, in this system, public interest is more important because it affects voter turnout. Therefore, governments and candidates for office must work harder to sway the opinions of voters. Second, people should be free to protest an election by refraining from taking part. Indeed, the very idea of forcing constituents to vote runs counter to the principles upon which free society is based.

Skill B

Q3 – practice 1

Step 1

Suggested answers:

The problem: woman can't use scholarship to study abroad

Man's opinion of policy: arbitrary and unfair
— Reason 1: woman earned her scholarship (not athletic or need-based)
— Reason 2: woman qualified for need-based, but chose academic scholarship instead

Step 3

Sample response:

The man's opinion is that the school's policy of only allowing students with need-based scholarships to use that money toward the Study Abroad Program is unfair. To begin, he contends that the woman earned her scholarship through academic merit rather than athletic skill or financial need. Secondly, the woman did qualify for a need-based scholarship but opted for the academic one, showing that she has the same financial need as students with need-based scholarships. For these two reasons, he feels the woman should be allowed to use her grant money to pay for tuition abroad.

Q3 – practice 2

Step 1

Suggested answers:

Woman's opinion:
— lottery system is unfair

Why:
— gives preferential treatment but should be based on need
— will cost her a lot of money for rent and transportation
— she won't be able to study late at the library

What university should have done:
— done construction in summer or made arrangements for students

Step 3

Sample response:

The woman is angry about the announced plan for a housing lottery for graduate students. First, she thinks it is unfair because students of certain majors are being given priority. Instead, she believes the housing should be assigned based on need. Second, she is upset because living off campus will be expensive and inconvenient. For example, she will pay more in rent and transportation and will not be able to study late on campus. In the end, she complains that they should have done the renovations during the summer or otherwise accommodated the needs of all students.

Q4 – practice 1

Step 1

Suggested answers:

Morphology of giant squid:
— length: 10-15 meters
— appendages: 8 arms, 2 tentacles
— suckers: have sharp, claw-like components

Theories on feeding behavior:
— passive reason: large body requires too much energy to move quickly
— active reasons: i) tentacles have claw-like parts suggesting capture of prey
ii) smaller squid species are active feeders

Step 3

Sample response:

The reading passage describes the morphological differences between marine animals that are active feeders and passive feeders. The lecturer examines the morphology of the giant squid and different theories about its feeding habits. First, the giant squid is a very large creature. Second, it has two tentacles that include sharp, claw-like components. Some scientists have postulated that the enormous size of the giant squid suggests it must be a passive feeder. Other scientists, in contrast, point to its tentacles and the model of smaller squid species as evidence suggesting that the giant squid is an active feeder.

Q4 – practice 2

Step 1

Suggested answers:

Early 20th Century: uproar in music world
 — reaction to new style of music
 — music fans criticized composers
 — composers called fans uncouth
Atonal music
 — used chromatic scale
 — contained 12 notes

Step 3

Sample response:

The professor begins by describing the negative response many early-20th-century audiences had to the advent of atonal musical forms. Listeners found the new style too unstructured in comparison to the traditional forms they were used to. As the reading passage describes, traditional European music was based on principles of melody. This music utilized the major and minor scales to produce the desired emotions. As the professor points out, atonal compositions utilized the chromatic scale rather than the major or minor scales. The chromatic scale includes 12 notes, all the notes a person can play on the piano.

Skill C

Q5 – practice 1

Step 1

Suggested answers:

Problem:	The man needs to use the gym, but won't have access until his student loan arrives.
Solution 1:	use the gym as a guest of a friend
Advantages:	can continue training
Disadvantages:	costs money each time; is inconvenient
Solution 2:	talk to coach and arrange a temporary card
Advantages:	save money and don't need a host
Disadvantages:	the coach is away

Step 2

Suggested answers:
1. The man cannot access the gym to work out because his student loan has not come through yet.
2. He should find a friend with access to the gym to act as a host.
3. His friend can give him access to the gym, and they can work out together.

Step 3

Sample response:

The man's problem is that he cannot access the gym to work out because his student loans have not come through to pay his tuition. The woman suggests two solutions to his problem. First, he could find a student with access to accompany him to the gym. Second, he could talk to his coach and try to get a temporary ID. In my opinion, the first choice is preferable. To begin, his coach is away, so the man would have to wait. In addition, having a friend to work out with could help him maintain his exercise regime.

Q5 – practice 2

Step 1

Suggested answers:

Problem:	The man wants to drop a class, but he has missed the deadline.
Solution 1:	drop the class
Advantages:	can concentrate on other subjects
Disadvantages:	dropping is same as failing
Solution 2:	don't drop the class
Advantages:	with hard study, could earn an OK grade
Disadvantages:	will be difficult and distract from other classes

Step 2

Suggested answers:
1. The man is behind in a class and wants to drop it, but dropping now would be the same as failing the class.
2. He should drop the class.
3. It would be better to concentrate on getting strong grades in the courses of his major.

Step 3
Sample response:

The man's problem is that he wants to drop the professor's class because he is too far behind to earn a high grade. In addition, the deadline for dropping classes without penalty has passed. The professor tries to convince him to remain in the class and work hard to increase his grade. In my opinion, he would be better off dropping the class. Even though he will be penalized for dropping the class the same as if he had failed it, he will benefit by being able to concentrate his efforts on the courses of his major.

Q6 – practice 1

Step 1
Suggested answers:

Main topic of lecture: changing music of the 20th century
— Origins of jazz and blues: in New Orleans; African Americans mixed African rhythms with European melodies
— Initial reactions: not accepted by most Americans; too wild, unstructured
— When became accepted: after white musicians used it in rock 'n' roll
— New forms today: still meet resistance; ex. hip-hop

Step 2
Suggested answers:
1. The advent of jazz had the most influence on modern popular music.
2. It brought new rhythms and scales to popular music.
3. It became accepted when white musicians used these forms in rock 'n' roll music.

Step 3
Sample response:

According to the lecture, the advent of jazz music had a significant influence on the trajectory of popular music over the past 100 years. To begin, it was developed by African Americans combining African rhythms with European melodies. In addition, jazz influenced the development of blues, which added an extra note to the major scale, thus creating the blues scale. At first, these musical forms were met with resistance. Later, however, they became widely accepted after being incorporated into rock 'n' roll music by white musicians such as Elvis Presley. Furthermore, they have influenced the form of more recent popular music styles, such as hip-hop.

Q6 – practice 2

Step 1
Suggested answers:

Main topic of lecture: the changing definition of the family
— Traditional conception of family: included man, woman, and 2.5 children, with man working outside the house and woman inside
— Those outside this conception: were marginalized and considered sick or unstable in some way
— Today's families: only 11-15 percent conform to traditional definition
— Universal aspects of family: intersection between making a society and making new people; it provides ideas of normal and natural

Step 2
Suggested answers:
1. The traditional conception of the family includes a working father, a domestic mother, and two or three children all living together in one home.
2. In the past, families that differed from this ideal were marginalized and considered flawed or unhealthy.
3. In all societies, the family helps define what is normal and natural.

Step 3
Sample response:

In this lecture, the professor examines the idea of family. The traditional ideal of the family includes a working father, a domestic mother, and two or three children all living together in one home. Furthermore, families that differed from this ideal were marginalized and considered flawed or unhealthy in the past. These days, however, only a minority of families conform to this ideal. In point of fact, the professor relates that the ideal defined a generation or two ago is only one step on an ever-evolving sequence of ideals. Finally, the professor states that in all societies, the family helps define what is normal and natural.

Vocabulary Review

Review 1

1. (B)	2. (D)	3. (A)
4. (A)	5. (B)	6. (D)
7. (A)	8. (B)	9. (A)
10. (D)	11. (B)	12. (A)
13. (D)	14. (A)	15. (C)
16. (C)	17. (B)	18. (A)
19. (D)	20. (B)	21. (D)
22. (D)	23. (B)	24. (A)
25. (C)	26. (A)	27. (B)
28. (D)	29. (C)	30. (A)
31. fellow	32. symbiotic	33. fostered
34. unparalleled	35. forged	36. diverse
37. indigenous	38. invaluable	39. swayed
40. milieu	41. innovation	42. endangered
43. diverse	44. afford	45. obligatory
46. (O)	47. (S)	48. (O)
49. (S)	50. (O)	

Review 2

1. (C)	2. (A)	3. (D)
4. (B)	5. (A)	6. (C)
7. (B)	8. (B)	9. (A)
10. (A)	11. (B)	12. (C)
13. (D)	14. (D)	15. (A)
16. (B)	17. (A)	18. (D)
19. (C)	20. (D)	21. (A)
22. (B)	23. (D)	24. (A)
25. (A)	26. (B)	27. (B)
28. (D)	29. (B)	30. (D)
31. indigenous	32. elusive	33. myriad
34. in vain	35. specimens	36. lambaste
37. glean	38. convey	39. Optimists
40. mainstream	41. over	42. in
43. by	44. in	45. off
46. (D)	47. (B)	48. (E)
49. (A)	50. (C)	

Chapter 3

Focus A

Step 1 Sentence stress on content words

Suggested answers:
1. <u>Before</u> that, I spent <u>hours</u> in the <u>library</u> doing <u>research</u>.
2. My <u>life</u> was <u>changed</u> by an <u>unexpected</u> <u>blizzard</u>.
3. In addition, they provide <u>counselors</u> who help <u>troubled</u> <u>youths</u> with <u>problems</u>.
4. I believe that <u>childhood</u> is an <u>integral period</u> in a <u>person's life</u>.
5. <u>Public schools</u>, on the other hand, <u>can</u> and <u>do provide</u> this <u>setting</u>.
6. That's more <u>captivating</u> and <u>educational</u> than looking at <u>pictures</u> or <u>reading texts</u>.
7. I prefer the <u>system</u> in which <u>voting</u> is <u>optional</u>.
8. <u>Instead</u>, she believes the <u>housing</u> should be assigned <u>based on need</u>.

Suggested clear words in **bold:**
I believe zoos serve a **multitude** of **useful purposes**. For one thing, zoos **educate** visitors. If there were no zoos, children would grow up **never witnessing** species **not indigenous** to their area. With zoos, in contrast, **children** can **learn** about **all kinds** of **different** animal species and **observe** them up close. That's more **captivating** and **educational** than looking at **pictures** or **reading texts**. For that matter, zoos provide an **entertainment** venue for people of **all ages**. Additionally, they provide a **safe home** for animals whose survival is **threatened in the wild**. Animals that are endangered can be **protected, well-fed**, and **encouraged** to breed.

Step 2 Sentence stress on function words

1. (S)   2. (S)   3. (R)
4. (R)   5. (S)   6. (S), (S)
7. (R)   8. (S)

1. That **isn't his** dog, <u>it's</u> **her** dog.
2. Most students **didn't** pass <u>the</u> exam, but John **did**.
3. She <u>likes</u> jazz music, <u>and</u> he likes blues music. I like jazz **and** blues music.
4. Kim **hasn't** paid <u>her</u> tuition fees, but Rick **has**.

5. The major scale **doesn't** have 12 notes, <u>but</u> the chromatic scale **does**.
6. Off-campus housing **isn't** just expensive; <u>it's</u> expensive **and** inconvenient.
7. **He** <u>didn't</u> get the need-based scholarship. **She** did.
8. You <u>can</u> take English 201 **or** English 205. You can't take both.

Focus B

Step 1 Changing pitch for emphasis

1. <u>Children</u> should attend school.
   a. Adults should work.
2. This experience helped tremendously with <u>my</u> studies.
   b. Unfortunately, it didn't help with her studies.
3. Subsequent developments in <u>pop</u> music were generally met with the same disapproval.
   b. Developments in classical music, on the other hand, were embraced in a short time.
4. Do you play on the varsity <u>basketball</u> team?
   a. No, I play on the hockey team.

1. I don't <u>abhor</u> jazz music. I don't really enjoy it that much, though.
2. <u>Her</u> behavior is antisocial. He is actually a nice guy.
3. The squid doesn't have <u>eight</u> appendages. It has ten.
4. <u>Jellyfish</u> drift with ocean currents. Squid use their arms to swim.
5. There is a glitch with her <u>computer</u>. Her phone is working fine.
6. The campus <u>renovations</u> will begin in September. The campus celebrations begin in October.

Step 2 Commas and series with *and* or *or*

1. Many of the most popular bands on the charts today are born from influences of rock, /(↗) hip-hop, /(↗) reggae, /(↗) ska, /(↗) and techno. (↘)
2. They were considered troubled, /(↗) pathological, /(↗) or dysfunctional. (↘)

3. I doubt it'll cover the cost of renting a place in this city, /(↗) especially near the campus. (↘)
4. Most giant squid are smaller, /(↗) growing to approximately ten meters. (↘)
5. European concert-goers were plugging their ears, /(↗) walking out on performances, /(↗) and muttering to themselves.(↘)
6. The chromatic scale simply means all the notes you can play on a piano, /(↗) without any notes left out.(↘)

Focus C

Step 1   Timing

1. The traditional ideal of the family includes a working father, / a domestic mother, / and two or three children all living happily in one home.
2. As it turned out, / he was a Chinese student trying to practice English.
3. After the Internet came into widespread use, / however, / I didn't have to go to the library at all.

4. Within minutes, / there was a raging blizzard.
5. Some alarmists contend that this is a fundamental societal problem, / a breakdown in values that will produce immeasurable negative effects.
6. These, / I believe, / are the most important skills learned at school.

1. The man's opinion is that the school's policy / of only allowing students with need-based scholarships to use that money toward the Study Abroad Program / is unfair.
2. To begin, / he contends that the woman earned her scholarship through academic merit / rather than athletic skill or financial need.
3. Secondly, / the woman did qualify for a need-based scholarship / but opted for the academic one, / showing that she has the same financial need as students with need-based scholarships.
4. For these two reasons, / he feels the woman should be allowed to use her grant money to pay for tuition abroad.

Question 1

Some people trust first impressions, while others prefer to get to know someone before making judgments. I used to trust first impressions, but now I do not. When I was working as a waiter at a cafe, I saw a man with worn-out clothes and really messy hair. He looked like a beggar, but then he sat down at a table. I told him I was sorry but he couldn't rest in the restaurant. It turned out that the man was a famous artist waiting for the director of a local museum. I was very embarrassed, and now I do not trust first impressions.

Question 2

Sample response 1:
I agree with the statement that people should only read books about real events, real people, and established facts. First, reading about legends or unproven claims only creates confusion and argument between people. Second, reading works of fiction only uses up time that could be spent learning about the world or real things. After all, there is more than enough to learn about the real world to keep people busy. Finally, getting too involved in works of fiction can damage a person's social skills and interest in interacting with others.

Sample response 2:
I disagree with the statement that people should only read books about real events, real people, and established facts. For one thing, it is not always clear which books are about real events and which are not. For instance, a religion may consider its holy book to be objective fact, or a country might consider its history books to be objective fact, while others, of course, do not. In addition, works of fiction spark the imagination and help people develop and grow in a way that non-fiction simply cannot.

Question 3

In the woman's opinion, the Career Services Center is a great place. She describes several ways that the center has helped her. First, she details how a counselor there helped her choose her major area of study. By using a series of tests of interests and abilities, he advised her to major in statistics or accounting. Second, she tells how the center can help students find jobs after graduation. They maintain a database of job and internship listings that students can read in order to find career opportunities. In the end, she recommends the man visit the center.

Question 4

Both the reading and the lecture are about the Earth's layers. The reading says that there are four layers. Those are the core, the mantle, the crust — uh, the core actually has two parts: the inner core and outer core. But the woman says that there are extra parts of the crust. I mean, the crust should really be thought of as having two parts, not just one. Those two parts are the continental crust and the oceanic crust. Then, she also goes on to explain some of the differences between the two parts of the crust. She mentions things like where they are located, how thick they are, and what they are made of. Anyway, the key point that she adds to the information in the reading is that the crust really has two parts.

Question 5

Sample response 1:
The two students discuss the man being put on academic probation. Because he chose to take too many courses and then became sick, he failed a geology class. Two possible solutions to his problem are discussed. The first option is to appeal the probation. The second option is to take the class again. In my opinion, the first option is the better of the two. Since the man does have extenuating circumstances surrounding his low grade, I think there is a good chance he could have the probation revoked. Thus, his failure would not appear on his records.

Sample response 2:
The two students discuss the man being put on academic probation. Because he chose to take too many courses and then became sick, he failed geology class. Two possible solutions to his problem are discussed. The first option is to appeal the probation. The second option is to take the class again. In my opinion, the second option is the better of the two. Since the man doesn't have a good excuse for his failure, he should retake the course within a year and work hard to earn a high grade. Thus, his failure would not appear on his records.

Question 6

In the lecture, the professor explains traditional Chinese medicine. First, he describes the theory of "chi," a form of energy that flows through paths in the body. In addition, he states that chi can be hot or cold. Chinese medicine contends that a healthy body maintains clear paths for the flow of chi as well as a balance between hot and cold forms. Unhealthy blockages or imbalances can arise through diet, body position, and mental stress. The professor also explains how Chinese medicine seeks to treat the cause of the problem rather than the symptoms. One form of treatment is the use of different herbs to manipulate chi.